**Advance praise for *Just Begin*:**

"Maybe the best advice for those who want to weave spirituality into their lives—whether meditation, prayer, or anything else—is to *Just Begin*. In this work, subtitled *A Sourcebook of Spiritual Practices*, religious studies professor Dann E. Wigner introduces 40 different practices from Eastern and Western traditions—from mindfulness to music, yoga to the Lord's Prayer. There are plenty of choices, if we can only begin."

*—Publishers Weekly*

"Dann Wigner offers a contemporary updating of classic Christian practices that can help Jesus' followers actually *live* the life he promised. Practicing these exercises with the flexibility Wigner suggests leads toward the 'union with God' that *is* the Jesus life. Quoting Merton, Wigner reminds us that we're all *beginners* who must begin every day *doing* what helps us *become* who we want to be tomorrow."

—Dr. Fred Meeks, Emeritus Professor of Religion,
Wayland Baptist Seminary

"In a world in which, as Dann Wigner puts it, 'motion is our default setting,' pausing to engage in spiritual practices can seem like an impossible task. Yet God desires relationship and promises to meet us as we are. With *Just Begin*, Dann Wigner deconstructs twenty-five spiritual practices into a 'how-to guide,' lowering the hurdle for beginners by describing each practice in simple language appropriate for people of all ages. Wigner even anticipates common questions of beginners. Spiritual directors, Christian educators, school chaplains, and anyone leading a community of faith will want to have at least two copies—one to have and one to lend. *Just Begin* is a welcomed addition to any library of books about spiritual practices. As Wigner invites his readers, find the one or ones that resonate with you and 'just begin.'"

—Jenifer C. Gamber, Assistant to the Rector and Day School Chaplain
at St. Patrick's Episcopal Church in Washington, D.C.

"Dann Wigner's insights as a religious studies scholar who practices what he preaches make *Just Begin* an essential guide for opening up centuries' worth of spiritual practices for those seeking wisdom in the present day. This book has just the right blend of gentle guidance and practical advice for the next steps on your spiritual journey."

—Gladys Ganiel, Queens University Belfast, Ireland

"*Just Begin* is author Dann Wigner's admonition to those who ponder adding a spiritual discipline to their daily schedules. *Just Begin* is written as a resource. Dr. Wigner has found just the right approach to surveying the spiritual disciplines. The book is full of wit, wisdom, and wonder. I anticipate using it as a teaching tool and as a personal reference in my daily practice."

—The Rev. Pat Russell, Spiritual Director

"Ready to live more fully? Dann Wigner's book, *Just Begin: A Sourcebook of Spiritual Practices*, opens doors to deeper intimacy with oneself, others, and God. This book is beautifully balanced, includes a wide range of spiritual practices, and encourages readers to adapt these to their own preferences. The greatest quality of Dann's book is its accessibility and value to all of us in our various stages of spiritual development. So let's get this treasure and just begin!"

—The Rev. Dr. Madoc Thomas, pastor of New Home
United Methodist Church, Lubbock, Texas

"*Just Begin* is about discovery, meaning, and grace. Through a variety of spiritual practices, you are invited into stillness and quiet. In these open spaces of time and rhythm, you can listen to your soul and encounter the whisper of God. For this contemplative person, the book was an amazing guide to options that invite one to go deeper and to just 'be' in the presence of our God!"

—Cookie Cantwell, Youth Ministries Coordinator, St. James Parish,
Wilmington, North Carolina

# Just Begin

A Sourcebook of Spiritual Practices

Dann E. Wigner

CHURCH
PUBLISHING
INCORPORATED

Church Publishing
19 East 34th Street
New York, NY 10016
www.churchpublishing.org

Cover design by Marc Whitaker, MTWdesign
Typeset by Rose Design

Library of Congress Cataloging-in-Publication Data

Names: Wigner, Dann E., author.
Title: Just begin : a sourcebook of spiritual practices / Dann E. Wigner.
Description: New York : Church Publishing, 2018. | Includes bibliographical
  references.
Identifiers: LCCN 2018014394 (print) | LCCN 2018034456 (ebook) | ISBN
  9781640650633 (ebook) | ISBN 9781640650626 (pbk.)
Subjects: LCSH: Spiritual life--Christianity.
Classification: LCC BV4501.3 (ebook) | LCC BV4501.3 .W54244 2018 (print) |
  DDC 248.4/6--dc23
LC record available at https://lccn.loc.gov/2018014394

ISBN-13: 978-1-64065-062-6 (pbk.)
ISBN-13: 978-1-64065-063-3 (ebook)

Printed in the United States of America

# Contents

# SECTION 4: SENSING / 91

# SECTION 5: EMBODYING / 129

# Acknowledgments

MANY PEOPLE HAVE BEEN MORE IMPORTANT than they will ever know to the production of this book. Still, I would like to name a few that were indispensable along the way. First, I offer my thanks to the persons who I have talked to face-to-face over the years or who visited my website (*www. dannwigner.com*). They often expressed confusion about where to begin with spirituality and thought the whole big mess of it was hopelessly complicated. This book is for you. Here is a place to begin. Second, I am ever so grateful that my publisher, Church Publishing Incorporated, and my editor, Sharon Ely Pearson, saw potential in this idea. Third, I appreciate the essential feedback of implementation provided by the groups who have invited me to workshop the practices contained in these pages, particularly St. Stephen's Episcopal Church (Lubbock, Texas), Christ Church Episcopal (South Pittsburg, Tennessee), and the Companions in Ministry group at the School of Theology of the University of the South. Fourth, I am thankful to those who read this manuscript in whole or in part and offered critical feedback and constructive criticism, especially Sean Ditmore and my wife, Leann Wigner. Fifth, I have to offer even more appreciation to Leann for tireless help in offering substantive aid in all editing and proofreading matters as well as arguing with me when I have "great ideas" that turn out to be wrong. Sometimes, I don't know why you put up with me, but I am glad that you do.

# Introduction

The greatest adventure is always right in front of us—in the realization that there is far more to the universe than what we see with our own two eyes. But how will we live into that adventure? That's where spiritual practices give us a place to begin.

## WHAT IS THIS BOOK?

What you are holding in your hands is not a novel, textbook, manual, or an answer to all of life's problems. This book is a sourcebook of spiritual practices. In the following pages, I will briefly introduce many practices to you. These introductions have one singular point: to begin. I am giving you enough information to begin to use each practice; what you do with each practice from that point is entirely up to you. Feel free to skip practices or entire chapters that do not appeal to you. Think of this book a bit like a dictionary or encyclopedia. It's not necessary to read straight through; rather, use it as needed.

## HOW IS THIS BOOK SET UP?

Since this book is a practical tool, you'll find that each chapter's layout is remarkably similar. Each chapter has five parts: (1) some brief background to the practice, (2) a step-by-step method to begin the practice, (3) many variations of the practice, (4) common questions and troubleshooting, and (5) some potential journaling prompts or discussion questions. The chapters themselves are arranged in sections that focus on basic areas of human experience in which the differing practices fit.

The first section is concerned with practices of meditating or concentrating deeply. On the basis of concentration, I then move to practices of contemplating or listening. These spiritual practices are helpful for quieting our minds of internal chatter and distraction. From the standpoint of listening, the third section of being is where I will introduce you to several practices that encourage us simply to be present wherever we are right now. That goal can be harder than you think. If you don't believe me, then try some of the practices from that section. Fourth, I draw together skills from meditating, listening, and being to the world around us through the language of sensing, specifically using our five senses to engage our world spiritually. Finally, I deal with practices of embodying which I have grouped together into several body "flows" with which you can experiment. Within this framework, I encourage you to remember a couple of important disclaimers.

Do not limit yourself by following the steps of each practice to the letter. I've provided steps so that you have somewhere to start. Please feel free to modify them to suit your individual needs and tastes. Second, the spiritual life and walking with God is not a series of steps. While a plan helps you to get started, God will often work outside the bounds of any practice detailed in these pages. Be open to the unpredictable. Third, if you are experimenting with a new type of practice, then try at least a few variations to see if that practice resonates with you. And don't feel bad that they don't all offer what you need spiritually. There are many practices in these pages that do not speak much to me personally. That's okay; variety is the spice of life after all. When you do find a practice or set of practices that connect with you, go ahead and seek out the additional resources that I have noted. These books are specifically chosen to go further in depth into the theory and implementation of each practice.

## WHY THIS BOOK?

At this early point, you might already be thinking, "Why another book on spiritual practices or spiritual disciplines? What makes this one special?" There are quite a few books out there. Most of these books focus on a few practices, at most ten to twelve. These practices are typically considered in great depth and often are organized around a central theme. In my experience, these books are often imposing and confusing. The average person leaves them with bewilderment or a sense of self-defeat in not attaining to the level of "true" spirituality. I seek to offer an alternative to that mentality. Adapt. Experiment. TRY. If you don't connect with a particular practice, do not feel defeated, simply feel human. This sourcebook is intended to be a reference tool for you, the person interested in prayer and spirituality, so you can add new methods and exercises to your mystical "toolbox" to enrich your spiritual life. And, like a toolbox, if you find that a particular screwdriver, hammer, or ratchet doesn't suit your needs, then there is no problem with finding a different one—the right tool for the right job.

## WHAT ABOUT ME?

One of the major reasons that I wanted to write this book for you is that I'm also writing it to me. I am not a "mystic" or "contemplative," and my life experiences have been fairly average. Yet I believe there is more to this world than we dare to think. Spiritual practices are a way to commit to that type of belief for me. In my own quest, I have studied and taught contemplative Christianity on academic and congregational levels, but—and I can't stress this enough—I know these practices as one who continually practices them—tweaking, refining, adapting, experimenting, learning, beginning again and again. I am a firm adherent to the perspective of which Thomas Merton articulated, "We do not want to be beginners. But let us be convinced of the fact that we will never be anything else but beginners all our life."[1]

So, let's begin . . .

---

1. Thomas Merton, *Contemplative Prayer* (Garden City, NY: Image Books, 1971), 37.

# Section 1

## MEDITATING

### WHAT IS MEDITATION?

In Christian history, if you wanted to think very deeply about God, a scripture passage, the universe, or other related subjects, then you would be talking about meditation or concentration. In fact, you can still find many books by holy men and women filled with statements and observations intended to encourage thought and reflection which are entitled "Meditations." If, however, you are thinking of meditation as a way to empty your mind of thoughts, then you will want to consult the section on being later in this book.

Many of the practices in this opening section easily fall under the moniker of concentration or repetition. I want to start here because I want us to start with the most familiar actions for any of us. We've all had to memorize or concentrate at one time or another in our lives. So, in that spirit, we'll take a look at the basics of getting started with some very traditional Christian practices: the Jesus Prayer, the Lord's Prayer, *lectio divina*, and the Spiritual Exercises of St. Ignatius of Loyola. Also, we'll investigate some potentially less familiar practices: reframing, observing, and journaling. These practices interact and arise from the traditions of mindfulness meditation. While we will look at mindfulness more in depth in the section on practices of being, I would like to introduce this way of spirituality briefly at this point.

Mindfulness arises from several mystical practices associated with the religions of the East. According to Susan Kaiser Greenland, in *Mindful Games*, "The word *mindfulness* comes from the ancient languages Sanskrit and Pali, in which it is defined as 'remembering'—as in remembering the object of our attention."[1] So we can see that mindfulness is closer to the Christian meaning of meditation than it might appear on the surface. While remembering, concentrating, or repeating may not be the most alluring activities when we think of spiritual practice, they are the foundation of all other practices. So let's get ready and stretch our concentration "muscles" as we begin.

---

1. Susan Kaiser Greenland, *Mindful Games: Sharing Mindfulness and Meditation with Children, Teens, and Families* (Boulder, CO: Shambhala, 2016), 53.

# 1

## The Jesus Prayer

### BRIEF BACKGROUND

The Jesus Prayer originated in the Eastern Orthodox tradition. While this practice has a long history, it is tied to the practices of early desert hermits, or *hesychasts*, in Egypt. In simplest terms, the Jesus Prayer as a practice is the activity of repeating over and over the prayer, "Jesus Christ, Son of God, have mercy on me, a sinner," or some close variant of these words. The purpose behind these repetitions may be driving out distracting thoughts or concentrating on the mercy of God. The number of repetitions varies greatly among practitioners, with some monastic adherents attempting to repeat this prayer mentally in a never-ending manner. This prayer can also be coupled in the Eastern Orthodox tradition with use of a prayer rope, similar to rosary beads, in which the person praying keeps count of the number of prayers by making or counting the number of knots in the rope.

### HOW TO PRACTICE

This practice is one of the simplest disciplines to begin, and it allows for endless variations.

1. Recite mentally or verbally, "Jesus Christ, Son of God, have mercy on me, a sinner."
2. Repeat.
3. Repeat.
4. Repeat.

There are no exact instructions for the exact number of times to recite this prayer or even how to do so in a specific way. When using the Jesus Prayer, you are trying to imprint Jesus Christ on your deepest thought patterns. The *hesychasts* considered this prayer as the path to literal adherence to St.

3

Paul's admonition to "pray without ceasing" (1 Thess. 5:17). You might like to jump right in, but if you are like me, you might want a few practical suggestions on how to implement this practice.

## VARIATIONS

### Synchronize with Your Breath

Try reciting a single phrase as you breathe in, then another while you breathe out. For example, "Jesus Christ," [breathe in] "Son of God," [breathe out] "have mercy on me," [breathe in] "a sinner" [breathe out]. You can vary this method even further. Try using only one word between breaths, or recite the entire prayer as you breathe deeply in or out.

### Different Words

If you consult some of the resources on the Jesus Prayer that I suggest, you'll notice that the exact words do vary a bit. For instance, try, "Lamb of God, who takes away the sin of the world, have mercy on me." You might also try varying your request. Instead of mercy, what else might you ask for? Grace? Hope? Patience? Peace?

### Mechanical Recitation

While I would not recommend this variation as your go-to method for the Jesus Prayer, think about simply reciting the words in your mind for a designated period of half an hour or hour. Do not take out any time set aside for the purpose of prayer. Just see what it's like to have those recurring words pounding into your subconscious mind again and again like a jackhammer.

### Word Meanings

Ruminate on the meaning of each word. "Jesus." What does that mean? "Christ." What does that mean? "Son." What does that mean? You can also use this variation with association by focusing on what other words come to mind as you repeat each word of the Jesus Prayer.

### Syllables

Break up your recitation to linger on specific syllables. Is that more distracting? Does it require more attention? Is there any meaning left when we break the words down into their constituent sounds? What might that teach us?

## Attitudes

Rather than varying the words, come at the recitation of words from different attitudes. Begin with the difference in saying the prayer between the Pharisee and tax collector (see Luke 18:9–14). How did you feel different when saying those words from different perspectives? How about different emotional states? Can you say the Jesus Prayer equally sincerely in a state of joy as in a state of abject demoralization? Journaling might be particularly useful here to help you differentiate among reactions.

## Switch

Imagine the prayer from Jesus' perspective, praying for you (see John 17). Try, "Father in heaven, have mercy on [your name], for I love them." What does it feel like to have Jesus pronounce your name?

## Back to Breath

As you breathe this prayer in and out, imagine that you are filled with the light and love of God as you inhale. Then imagine that all guilt, worry, and trouble flow out of you as you exhale.

Truthfully, the sky's the limit when it comes to variations of this practice. What are some other possibilities? What do you wish you could change about the prayer? Why not change it?

# COMMON QUESTIONS

**Q:** What if I've never practiced this type of prayer before?

**A:** First of all, go easy on yourself. Don't expect too much out of the practice until you get used to the "mechanics" of it. Also, realize that this type of prayer practice has results that are seen more in your attitude throughout the day rather than during the practice itself.

**Q:** What if I don't feel anything?

**A:** This is a common question that applies to almost any practice. Please rest assured that these practices are not about certain feelings. Feelings come and go. At times, you may have very intense feelings while praying the Jesus Prayer. At other times, you might not feel anything special at all. That's okay. Feelings will vary from time to time and from person to person. Find your own rhythm.

**Q:** Is there any relative difference between the effectiveness of saying the Jesus Prayer aloud versus saying it silently?

**A:** Not really. Speaking the prayer aloud often helps to focus your attention. Of course, there are some obvious circumstances in which you would not want to verbalize the prayer like walking down a crowded street or riding the bus, but there is no "spiritual" difference in verbalizing or not verbalizing the prayer.

**Q:** Are particular postures or gestures necessary when using the Jesus Prayer?

**A:** No, this prayer is very versatile. You can pray it kneeling, seated, prostrated, standing, walking, or even running. You can combine the prayer with the sign of the cross or even some of the yoga postures suggested in chapter 25.

**Q:** Do you need to have or make an Eastern Orthodox prayer rope to use with the Jesus Prayer?

**A:** While a prayer rope it is not essential, it is a very effective tool for keeping your hands focused in a complementary way to your mind as you repeat the Jesus Prayer. Rosary beads can also be used in the same way.

**Q:** Is the Jesus Prayer "magic"?

**A:** No, there is no ethereal "power" in the words themselves. Additionally, the mere repetition of the words does not guarantee some obligation on the part of God, like a "magic spell" is intended to produce. The Jesus Prayer is chiefly effective to change you, not God. God always wants to show mercy; we are just not always willing to seek and accept it.

**Q:** Is the Jesus Prayer a mantra?

**A:** If the Jesus Prayer had to be compared to another type of repetitive meditative practice, then a mantra would be the closest analog. However, they are not quite the same. The intended purpose of a mantra is to use the act of repetition itself to drive thoughts out of the practitioner's mind—to empty your thoughts. The Jesus Prayer works in the opposite direction. You are seeking to fill your mind with a constant awareness of Christ. While that process would also drive out spurious thoughts, the balance of emphasis has shifted.

**Q:** Is the Jesus Prayer an example of self-hypnosis or autosuggestion?

**A:** Much like the previous question, there are some points of contact between self-hypnosis and the Jesus Prayer. Both the psychological practice of self-hypnosis and the Jesus Prayer are focused on imprinting a particular thought pattern on the practitioner. However, you are entirely conscious when using the Jesus Prayer. You are not trying to engage your subconscious mind in the Jesus Prayer. So while self-hypnosis or autosuggestion is seeking to change a participant, the Jesus Prayer is a reminder about a commitment to change, that is, a commitment to seek and accept God's mercy.

**Q:** The Jesus Prayer seems very sin-focused. What if I don't feel the need to focus on sin in that way?

**A:** You might try a variant of the Jesus Prayer that focuses on a different aspect of God's action or nature like hope or love. Also, you might try conceiving of sin in terms of your "struggles" or "problems" rather than in terms of "transgressions" or even "temptations."

**Q:** Are there any circumstances in which the Jesus Prayer might be counterproductive?

**A:** Yes, if you suffer from obsessive compulsive disorder (OCD), then you might try a different prayer practice. The repetitive nature of the Jesus Prayer could reinforce OCD and detract from the good purposes of the practice itself.

**Q:** How similar is the Jesus Prayer to the Ave Maria ("Hail Mary") prayer which is used with the Catholic Rosary?

**A:** Both Eastern Orthodox prayer ropes and Catholic rosary beads are used in similar ways. While these two prayers are not exactly interchangeable, they are used in an analogous way. There is no problem at all if you wish to use the "Hail Mary" with a prayer rope or the Jesus Prayer with rosary beads.

## POTENTIAL JOURNALING PROMPTS OR DISCUSSION QUESTIONS

1. What positive experiences did you have while practicing this practice?
2. What negative experiences did you have while practicing this practice?
3. How did you adapt this structure to your situation?
4. How did you meet God in this practice?
5. How did the repetitive nature of this practice impact you?
6. How did the Jesus Prayer encourage you to think about mercy this week?
7. How did the physical act of using a prayer rope (if you did so) help you to pray this week?

# 2

---

# The Lord's Prayer

## BRIEF BACKGROUND

The Lord's Prayer (Matt. 6:9–13; Luke 11:2–4) is a very common prayer for Christians of all branches and denominations. We often say it in our services, we teach it to our children at bedtime, and we inscribe it in various artful ways around our homes. With any feature of our spirituality that is so ever-present, it might be easy for the Lord's Prayer to lose meaning as we repeat the words of it by rote. This practice helps us to slow down and pay attention to the words once again.

## HOW TO PRACTICE

1. First, you'll need to settle on a particular version of the prayer. If you know multiple languages, it may help to use the language that you are least familiar with in order to slow down your pace with the prayer. I've personally found value in using a German version of this prayer (which is my less familiar language). However, if you would like to use an English version, I recommend this one from the Book of Common Prayer, page 364:

   > Our Father, who art in heaven,
   > hallowed be thy Name,
   > thy kingdom come,
   > thy will be done,
   > on earth as it is in heaven.
   > Give us this day our daily bread.
   > And forgive us our trespasses,
   > as we forgive those

who trespass against us.
And lead us not into temptation,
but deliver us from evil.
For thine is the kingdom,
and the power, and the glory,
for ever and ever. Amen.

2. Sit or kneel down in a comfortable position. Gently close your eyes. Rest your hands on your knees, or bring them up into the traditional prayer posture with palms together. If you are having a hard time focusing, then gently fix your gaze as if you were looking at your nose while keeping your eyes closed. The stillness of your eyes will help to quiet your mind.

3. Say or think the first phrase of the prayer: "Our Father." Ponder on this phrase for five slow breaths. Try to call up an image in your mind to associate with this phrase. Use whatever image is personally meaningful to you; it does not have to fit any particular traditional imagery.

4. After five breaths, continue to the next phrase: "who art in heaven," and continue the process for each phrase throughout the course of the prayer.

5. While this practice may take a significant investment of time (twenty to thirty minutes), it bears fruit quickly by enriching the experience of reciting the Lord's Prayer when you do so more quickly in other contexts.

## VARIATIONS

If you find this practice personally meaningful, you might try connecting it with a hands-on method of praying. For instance, you might try going through the phrases with rosary beads in a similar manner to what I described for the practices of the Jesus Prayer. Experiment with different connections and find what works best for you.

## COMMON QUESTIONS

Q: Are there any differences among the Lord's Prayer, the Jesus Prayer, and the various prayers associated with the Rosary?

**A:** There is quite a bit of difference among the prayers concerning history of development, content, and even purpose. While the Lord's Prayer is much longer than the others, it is likely the one you know best. Also, many Christian churches use the Lord's Prayer often in their worship services. That liturgical setting shapes how you might want to view and use this prayer.

**Q:** Is it okay to have very odd imagery associated with particular phrases as I meditate on the Lord's Prayer?

**A:** Really, anything goes here, as long as it is personally meaningful and helpful to you as you focus on God.

**Q:** Is it okay to personalize the language a bit more? For instance, could I say "my father" instead of "our father"?

**A:** While it is fine to personalize the language, there is something to be said for "breathing" into the traditional wording that is already there. Personally, I have tried meditation with the Lord's Prayer using very contemporary Bible paraphrases, such as *The Message*, and I found that sometimes I focused more on the prayer and sometimes I just didn't quite connect. Experiment here. See what works for you.

**Q:** What if I feel like I'm just going through the motions—just repeating to repeat, so to speak?

**A:** I can almost guarantee that you will feel like that some of the time. That realization does not necessarily mean you should set the prayer aside; instead, realize that the recognition of how you have "wandered" into repeating by rote is a step on the way. Refocus your attention. Perhaps shift an image in your meditation or shift your physical posture. Try coming at the practice from a new angle before moving on to a new practice. Of course, no single prayer practice is the be-all and end-all of Christian prayer, not even this one. Feel free to try something else, but I advise you to first discern whether you might be only momentarily bored.

**Q:** What about theological differences in various wordings of the prayer (e.g., "trespasses" or "debts"; "temptation" or "trial")?

**A:** That sounds like an excellent subject to meditate on the next time you pray the Lord's Prayer. Are there differences in meaning for you with different wordings? Do those differences change how you perceive prayer? Or how you perceive God?

**Q:** Do I need to use the exact words of the prayer, or can I use the Lord's Prayer as a "model" which the Bible seems to advocate (see Matt. 6:9–13; Luke 11:2–4)?

**A:** It's up to you; however, I suggest sticking with some version of exact wording if you are intending to use the Lord's Prayer to help focus your attention on God. If you are thinking of how to form your own specific words according to the model of the Lord's Prayer within the prayer time, then you are distracting your attention through this thinking process. Memorization is an important tool in your toolbox for this practice.

**Q:** What if I am having problems looking at the Lord's Prayer in fresh ways because I am so familiar with this prayer?

**A:** In that case, you may want to consult some of the works in the "Resources for Further Study" section on page 201. Many of them attempt to come at the Lord's Prayer from less well-known perspectives.

## POTENTIAL JOURNALING PROMPTS OR DISCUSSION QUESTIONS

1. What positive experiences did you have while practicing this practice?
2. What negative experiences did you have while practicing this practice?
3. How did you adapt this structure to your situation?
4. How did you meet God in this practice?
5. How did the repetitive nature of this practice impact you?
6. What were some of the most meaningful or surprising image associations that came up as you prayed?
7. If you coupled this practice with rosary beads or a prayer rope, how did the physical activity impact your prayer?

# 3

## Lectio Divina

### BRIEF BACKGROUND

*Lectio divina*, which means "sacred/divine reading," is a mystic practice that specifically deals with sacred texts, principally the Bible. In this practice, you select a portion of a reading and then read through it multiple times. Each reading has a specific purpose beyond comprehending the historical meaning of the text. The practice helps you to meditate on scripture in order to meet God and/or gain insight. Please note that this chapter is laid out differently than other chapters. There are still five sections, but since we are really talking about one single, overarching practice in this chapter, the variations' section will be much more expansive.

### HOW TO PRACTICE

1. The first stage of the practice is *lectio* or "reading." In this stage, choose a scripture passage and read it slowly and repetitively. You may choose a different reading for each session.
2. The second step is *oratio* or "speaking." In this stage, read the passage aloud. Focus on what God is saying to you. Look for a specific word or phrase that stands out to you.
3. The third stage is *meditatio* or "meditation." In this stage, concentrate on the word or phrase that stood out to you when you were reading. Focus on how God could be speaking to you today through this word or phrase. You then end your prayer time with the Lord's Prayer or another personally meaningful prayer, and keep meditating on the word or phrase, which stood out to you from your reading throughout the day.
4. The final stage is *contemplatio* or "contemplation." This stage is something you cannot control. This is where God meets you, and it can happen any

time or anywhere. The process of *lectio* helps one to be attentive to those "eureka" moments when an insight strikes you suddenly because God is not necessarily limited to showing up in burning bushes.

# VARIATIONS

## With an Image

1. In the stage of *lectio*, choose a passage and read it through multiple times. Read it slowly and repetitively.

2. In the stage of *oratio*, read your passage aloud. Focus on an image or character rather than a word.

3. In the stage of *meditatio*, concentrate on this image. Flesh it out. Use all five senses if you can. Form the clearest picture of that image or character in your mind. End your prayer time with the request for help to hold that image in your mind throughout the day. Apply it to your everyday life.

4. In the stage of *contemplatio*, how is God speaking to you through this image? Nothing is too mundane or silly. What is God teaching you through this image? Speak that thought out loud. Write it down. Consider how you can integrate that insight into your life.

## Body

1. In the stage of *lectio*, read the "book" of your own body as the subject. Take a few moments. Focus on one of your five senses: sight, hearing, smell, taste, or touch.

2. In the stage of *oratio*, speak aloud what you are feeling through that sense right now. Be specific, even if you are feeling nothing out of the ordinary. What do you see? What do you hear? What do you smell? What can you taste or touch (these senses will require something to eat or handle)?

3. In the stage of *meditatio*, take a few moments to settle down. For five slow breaths (or more), really concentrate on the information coming through the sense you've chosen.

4. In the stage of *contemplatio*, hold in your mind throughout the day this question: "What is God telling me through my senses today?" You

might just be surprised at how much you pay attention to your body today instead of moving obliviously through the day expecting your body to just do its "job" while you are focused elsewhere.

*Note:* If you find value in this variation, you can also try different senses on different days or go through all five senses in a single day. Experiment. See what works for you.

## Memories

1. In the stage of *lectio*, sift through your memories—recent or long-term—until a particular event stands out to you. It doesn't have to be especially spiritual, just memorable to you in this moment.

2. In the stage of *oratio*, speak out loud, or perhaps write, the event as you remember it. Try to tell the "story" of it as if you were speaking to an impartial third party. Focus on verbalizing every possible detail to create the fullest picture that you can recall.

3. In the stage of *meditatio*, close your eyes, and replay the event in your mind. Remember how you were there, but don't be afraid to use your imagination. Try and replay events from any other people in the memory. What might have been their perspectives? Ponder on why this specific memory came to you when you settled down today to practice *lectio*.

4. In the stage of *contemplatio*, carry this memory with you today. It might even help to carry a tangible reminder of that memory, some memento if possible. If not, find something to help remind you. If all else fails, you can try the old method of tying a string around your finger to remind yourself. Ask God what the past has to teach you about him today. You might be surprised at how much a little attention can change something as simple as remembering.

## Wandering

1. In the stage of *lectio*, take a word or phrase that stands out to you in a scripture or other spiritual reading.

2. In the stage of *oratio*, think out loud (if possible) of how that word or phrase can ground you in your own experience right now.

3. In the stage of *meditatio*, take some time just to walk. While you wander with your feet, also wander into the uncomfortable place of how that word or phrase might unsettle your comfortable routines and call you to something deeper.

3. In the stage of *contemplatio*, stop and wonder at what new and amazing place God might be drawing you toward by pointing out that word or phrase to you today. Try to hold this deliberate attitude of wonder before you as you go through your day today.

*Note:* If possible, wander out in nature. It is often the best place to find God—and yourself.

## Journaling

1. Do you like to write? If so, in the stage of *lectio*, take a word or phrase that stands out to you as you read a passage of some work for spiritual enrichment.

2. In the stage of *oratio*, instead of verbalizing, take some time just to write down the word or phrase over and over. Try to write it as deliberately as you can. Try different styles of writing. Print. Cursive. Calligraphy, if you feel whimsical. Perhaps write it in different languages. Get a feel for this word and phrase.

3. In the stage of *meditatio*, try journaling with the word or phrase. You can connect it to your own experience and journal about your thoughts and feelings, or you can let your imagination go wild and use that word or phrase to create an entirely new story. It doesn't have to be tied to the original spiritual passage at all. The act of creation is inherently spiritual. It doesn't have to be limited to religious subjects.

3. In the stage of *contemplatio*, hold the results of your journaling in your mind and heart along with the simple prayer: "Teach me." See what God has to say through your own journaling.

*Note:* For a little added bonus, write out your journaling for the day in a letter format and mail it to yourself. That will give you a little more time to ponder and mull over the content before receiving the letter back in the mail in a day or two.

## Creative

1. In the stage of *lectio*, take a word or phrase that stands out to you in a scripture or other spiritual reading.

2. In the stage of *oratio*, take that word or phrase and decide on a creative method to explore and express the meanings, thoughts, and feelings behind that word or phrase. Do you like to paint? draw? sing? dance? compose poetry?

3. In the stage of *meditatio*, create according to the words and methods you have chosen. Remember that your word or phrase is only a starting point. There is no specific plan you have to follow or particular outcome that must result. Use the creative process itself as a form of prayer.

4. In the stage of *contemplatio*, take a step back from whatever you have created (metaphorically speaking if you have chosen a performance-based art). Ponder on how God's Spirit moved through you to create. The result is not as primary here as the process. Hold that insight in your mind as well.

*Note:* I have had some participants mention that they found great enjoyment in using a creative method that was new and unfamiliar to them. If you are an accomplished hand at painting or a practiced poet, then branch out. Stretch yourself.

## Music

1. In the stage of *lectio*, choose a musician or song that is meaningful to you and listen to it. Listen to the song multiple times. Try to listen carefully for a word or phrase that stands out to you. With most music, if no word or phrase stands out, then you can always rely on the chorus for inspiration.

2. In the stage of *oratio*, speak aloud this word, phrase, or refrain. If you are musically inclined, you might try singing it yourself, perhaps in different styles and arrangements. Remember that this stage is about verbalizing and imprinting this word or phrase on your ears, lips, heart, and mind.

3. In the stage of *meditatio*, continue what you began in *oratio*. You might also add other recordings of this song in different arrangements or

by different artists. Hopefully, you will get the song, words, or phrase "stuck" in your head and ears for the rest of the day.

4. In the stage of *contemplatio*, carry this newly created "earworm" with you as you go throughout your day. If the situation allows, hum along, tap your foot, get the rest of your body into the act of *lectio* here too. Ponder what God may be teaching you through these songs, and try to go beyond any obvious connections too. Music evokes emotion. What emotions might God be using to speak to you?

## TV or Movies

1. In the stage of *lectio*, select a movie or TV show to watch for the express purpose of spiritual enrichment. It doesn't need to be an obviously "spiritual" movie. God may speak to you more through *Groundhog Day* or *The Avengers* than through *The Passion of the Christ*. I know that God does to me.

2. In the stage of *oratio*, pray a short prayer like: "God, show me something about your truth in what I watch." Then start watching the show.

3. In the stage of *meditatio*, pay attention as you watch. What might God be telling you through a character, sequence of events, setting, symbol, or snippet of dialogue? If need be, write down what stands out to you for further reflection after the show.

4. In the stage of *contemplatio*, keep what you saw on your mind. Rewatch the show, if you can. However, I personally tend to practice this form of *lectio* when I go to watch movies in the cinema. I find that the all-encompassing environment makes it easier to concentrate. Also, remember that it might be the little things that strike you. God works mysteriously, and God might even get our attention through the most unlikely ways.

*Note:* As another variation, I like to combine this method with the previous one and practice *lectio* with the soundtracks to certain movies. Whether the songs have words or are only instrumental, this is one of my favorite ways to "replay" a movie in my head to ponder the implications of the actions of characters in combination with the emotional responses that the accompanying music evokes.

## People

1. In the stage of *lectio*, look at other people. Friends. Family. Coworkers. Each person is a unique expression of God's image, and he or she is also a book of what God is doing on earth.

2. In the stage of *oratio*, don't speak. Listen. Listen to them. Really pay attention. What are they saying beneath the surface? Where is pain and difficulty for them? Where is joy and laughter?

3. In the stage of *meditatio*, ponder how God may speak to you through them. This step dovetails nicely with the practice of the presence of God, which will be detailed in chapter 12. If God is always present, are we paying attention to see him in others?

4. In the stage of *contemplatio*, continue what you first began in *meditatio*; ponder how God is speaking to you; and add one new perspective. Consider how you may be the word of God that they need to hear. Be more aware of what you say today, not just more aware of what you hear.

## COMMON QUESTIONS

**Q:** How large of a passage should I use?

**A:** The length of passage is really up to you. If you are using the Bible, I recommend using the section divisions available in most Bibles. In other words, you don't want to read more than one particular story or event. Collections of sayings could be limited to five to ten verses. You might also consider using the Daily Office to designate specific passages of scripture.

**Q:** Should I always use the Bible?

**A:** While this practice was developed with the Bible in mind, it is applicable to any book. You don't even need to limit *lectio* to traditionally spiritual works. You just want to choose something that holds deep meaning for you.

**Q:** What if an odd word or phrase stands out to me?

**A:** Then go with it. I have often had an odd word or phrase stand out to me. In fact, one time the only word that stood out to me in a rather lengthy passage was the word "if." So, I pondered on the word "if" for that day.

**Q:** What if an image or person stands out rather than a word?

**A:** This is a very common issue. While words tend to stand out to verbally focused people (such as myself), most people are more visually or relationally oriented. Ponder on that image or person.

**Q:** What if there isn't anything that stands out to me?

**A:** Believe it or not, this is actually my favorite question. If you practice *lectio* often, then you'll definitely run into this issue. You might try coming back to the passage later. If there still isn't anything that stands out to you, then ponder on how there is so much about God that goes beyond words and images. Also, don't be too hard on yourself. It's a bit like eating a meal. Eating is essential for us to live, but there are many meals that are not particularly memorable. "Chewing" on a spiritual writing is bound to meet with a similar result occasionally.

**Q:** Why is *lectio divina* sometimes called meditation?

**A:** In the Christian tradition, the word *meditation* has historically referred to thinking deeply on a doctrine, thought, experience, or scripture. In popular usage, the word *meditation* means something closer to what Christians mean by the terms *contemplation* or *illumination*.

**Q:** What if I feel like I'm picking and choosing words or phrases that stand out?

**A:** You may feel that way from time to time. I certainly do. That's okay. God can work through your own thought process too. If you feel that this is happening all the time, then maybe this practice is not the one that resonates with you most deeply. You might try some other practice from these pages. No worries. There is something here for everyone.

**Q:** How do I know that I've achieved the final stage of the practice?

**A:** The nature of faith is that we never fully know; we believe. If you feel that the word or phrase that stood out to you offered you some insight or strength for the day or week, then it "worked." There is no need to "chart" progress through these steps; God can work very subtly. The real answer to the practice is whether you found value in it or not. That's the essential piece.

## POTENTIAL JOURNALING PROMPTS
## OR DISCUSSION QUESTIONS

1. What positive experiences did you have while practicing this practice?
2. What negative experiences did you have while practicing this practice?
3. How did you adapt this structure to your situation?
4. What scripture(s) did you pray?  What word or phrase stood out to you?
5. How did praying scripture help you to connect to the characters of the Bible? How did praying scripture help you to listen to God?
6. How did you meet God in this practice?

# 4

## The Spiritual Exercises
## of St. Ignatius of Loyola

### BRIEF BACKGROUND

St. Ignatius of Loyola developed these spiritual exercises in the sixteenth century as the basis of spiritual development for initiates in his new order, the Society of Jesus, more commonly known as the Jesuits. For the time, these exercises were quite practical and concrete spiritual practices, and they continue to form the foundation for many contemplative retreats both inside and outside of the Jesuit order. The Examination (or *Examen*) is the central practice of these exercises, and it provides a way of taking stock of the sin in your life; it is often used independently of the rest of the exercises. Still, due to our present-day focus on shame, it may be difficult to see the value in the Examination and the other exercises.

In order to recapture the original spirit of the practice, I'm suggesting below a "translated" version of Ignatius' Exercises. The point we are seeking is that the struggles, difficulties, and weaknesses of our lives are the places that God can show up and bring change. Our struggles can be opportunities to get past our own self-importance in order to see God a little more clearly . . . if we'll allow it. If you do not feel like you have the significant time commitment recommended for all of the exercises, then just experiment with the Examination. See where it might lead you.

### HOW TO PRACTICE

#### The Examination

*Note:* If you are following the weekly schedule, then practice every day; multiple times a day, if possible. Five or ten minutes is usually enough time.

1. Take five deep breaths.
2. Pray: "Thank you, God, for breath today!"
3. Say, think, or write: "What am I struggling with today?"

   - Choices
   - Feelings (Emotions)
   - Thoughts
   - Sensations (Body)—i.e., sight, hearing, smell, taste, touch (What is your body telling you today?)

     o Are you tense, relaxed, happy, sad, angry, calm, energetic, exhausted, satisfied, discontent?
     o How might your choices, feelings, thoughts, and sensations connect to your struggles right now?

6. Pray: "God, I am struggling with _____ today. Help me in the way that you see is best."
7. Take five deep breaths.

## Conversations with Christ

With the meditation for each day, imagine yourself having a talk with Jesus about the passage or question on which you are thinking. Use your senses here: Are you walking with Jesus, standing, sitting? Where do the two of you meet? What do you see and hear around Jesus? What does Jesus look like? How does he talk to you? What is it like to have Jesus just listen to you? Try to picture the scene as fully in your head as possible. You may want to journal, write, draw, paint, talk out loud, e-mail, post to social media, walk in nature, gaze at the stars, or any other relaxing activity as you picture this "conversation" happening.

## VARIATIONS

These variations are arranged by week according to the themes set up by St. Ignatius. For this chapter, suggested journaling prompts and discussion questions are integrated into these weekly variations.

# Theme of the First Week: Sin

**Q:** "What is sin?

**A:** Sin is the seeking of our own will instead of the will of God, thus distorting our relationship with God, with other people, and with all creation."[1]

## Comments

Sin is a difficult topic to consider. Interestingly, sin is something that every person thinks about—at least from time to time—but no one really likes others to talk about. Sin may have an aspect of willful rebellion, but it also can simply mean a mistake, a struggle, a way that life falls short of perfection. To meditate on sin, we are not going to sit around with long faces, wailing about our wretchedness. Rather, we want to begin to approach God in humility. The point we are seeking is that the struggles, difficulties, and weaknesses of our lives are the places that God can show up and change. Our struggles can be opportunities to get past our own self-importance in order to see God a little more clearly . . . if we'll allow it.

### Day 1: Examination

Read: Genesis 1:27–28.

Ponder: Take a moment just to sit with the original goodness of humanity.

Read: Genesis 3:16–19

Ponder: What happened? Why move from goodness to evil so quickly?

[Conversations with Christ on this topic]

### Day 2: Examination

Read: Psalm 8:3–4.

Ponder: Who am I that God is mindful of me?

[Conversations with Christ on this topic]

### Day 3: Examination

Read: Job 38:1–11.

---

1. "An Outline of the Faith" in the Book of Common Prayer (New York: Church Hymnal Corporation, 1979), 848.

Ponder: Am I afraid to ask God questions? How much does fear keep me from saying how I really feel?

[Conversations with Christ on this topic]

### Day 4: Examination

Read: Luke 15:11–32.

Ponder: What does mercy look like to me?

[Conversations with Christ on this topic]

### Day 5: Examination

Read: Matthew 25:14–30.

Ponder: What will I do with the time that is given to me?

[Conversations with Christ on this topic]

## Ending Thought on Sin

Up to now human beings lived apart from each other, scattered around the world and closed in upon themselves. They have been like passengers who accidentally met in the hold of a ship, not even suspecting the ship's motion. Clustered together on the earth, they found nothing better to do than to fight or amuse themselves. Now, by chance, or better, as a natural result of organization, our eyes are beginning to open. The most daring among us have climbed to the bridge. They have seen the ship that carries us all. They have glimpsed the ship's prow cutting the waves. They have noticed that a boiler keeps the ship going and a rudder keeps it on course. And, most important of all, they have seen clouds floating above and caught the scent of distant islands on the horizon. It is no longer agitation down in the hold, just drifting along; the time has come to pilot the ship. It is inevitable that a different humanity must emerge from this vision. —Pierre Teilhard de Chardin[2]

Ponder: Where do we go from here?

## Potential Journaling Prompts or Discussion Questions on Sin

1. Is there some area of your life that needs healing? Can you tell God about it?

---

2. Pierre Teilhard de Chardin, *Activation of Energy* (New York: Harcourt Brace, 1971), 73–74.

2. Have you ever felt angry at God? Can you tell God that? If you have told God about your anger, how did God seem to react?

3. How much of your life is controlled by the motive of fear?

4. What does the word *sin* mean to you? How might it relate to anger, fear, and healing?

5. Are there resonances here with modern programs, e.g., the twelve-step program of Alcoholics Anonymous?

6. How do you react when you read the news? Should you talk to God about your reactions?

## Theme of the Second Week: Incarnation

"**Q:** What do we mean when we say that Jesus is the only Son of God?

**A:** We mean that Jesus is the only perfect image of the Father, and shows us the nature of God.

**Q:** What is the nature of God revealed in Jesus?

**A:** God is love.

**Q:** What do we mean when we say that Jesus was conceived by the power of the Holy Spirit and became incarnate from the Virgin Mary?

**A:** We mean that by God's own act, his divine Son received our human nature from the Virgin Mary, his mother.

**Q:** Why did he take our human nature?

**A:** The divine Son became human, so that in him human beings might be adopted as children of God, and be made heirs of God's kingdom.[3]"

### Comments

God became human. Those three words are the core of the Christian faith and message. The rest of the Bible, and particularly the Gospels, is answering the inevitable questions that follow that statement: Why? How? Where? When? What does that mean? Meditate on the life of Christ with these important questions in mind. While it might be tempting to skip ahead to consider Jesus' life in terms of his death, let's sit with

---

3. "An Outline of the Faith," in the Book of Common Prayer, 849–50.

how the life of Jesus displays the interplay of divinity and humanity in a unique way.

### Day 1: Examination

Read Luke 4:14–30.

Ponder: What would you think if a "local boy" came into church talking this way?

[Conversations with Christ on this topic]

### Day 2: Examination

Read Luke 9:57–10:12.

Ponder: Pick one of the unnamed "rejected" disciples. What would you do in their place? Why do you think Jesus was so harsh with them?

[Conversations with Christ on this topic]

### Day 3: Examination

Read Luke 12:16–21.

Ponder: Why would Jesus need a parable to talk about this topic? Is there any time that it is okay to keep what you have for yourself rather than give to others?

[Conversations with Christ on this topic]

### Day 4: Examination

Read Luke 6:20–26.

Ponder: Which blessing gives you the most hope? Why? Which woe scares you the most? Why?

[Conversations with Christ on this topic]

### Day 5: Examination

Read Luke 14:12–24.

Ponder: What do you think was going through the mind of the slave? Why?

[Conversations with Christ on this topic]

## Ending Thought on Incarnation: Making a Good Decision

Ignatius of Loyola offers some practical advice throughout the Exercises. For instance, he recommends two methods for making a good Christian decision:

### Method One

1. Put the choice clearly before your mind. Write it out, if necessary.
2. Remember your purpose in life: "the praise of God and the salvation of my soul."
3. Ask God to move your will to the right choice.
4. Think or write the advantages or benefits of each potential option.
5. Think or write the disadvantages or drawbacks of each potential option.
6. Consider what the most balanced action is—bringing in reason, emotion, other people's viewpoints, etc.
7. Make the decision, but continue to pray that this decision (the best one you could see) honors God.

### Method Two (for those really "thorny" dilemmas)

1. Put the choice before your mind. What would be the most loving thing to do?
2. What option would you advise someone else to do?
3. What option would you choose if this were your last day on earth?

Ponder: What decision have you been putting off? Run it through one or both of these methods. See what happens.

## Potential Journaling Prompts or Discussion Questions on Incarnation

1. Do you have any desire to get to know Jesus better? Do you want to desire a closer relationship with him? Can you tell him what your real desires are?
2. Can you truly believe that Jesus might want your friendship?
3. How do you answer Jesus' question, "Who do you say that I am" (Matt. 16:13)? Can you tell him who he is for you?
4. How is your life actually different because of what Jesus did two thousand years ago?
5. Why is Jesus' life (not considering death and resurrection) unique? What can you learn from him that will make a difference for you right here, right now?

## Theme of the Third Week: Sacrifice and Eucharist

**"Q:** What is the great importance of Jesus' suffering and death?

**A:** By his obedience, even to suffering and death, Jesus made the offering which we could not make; in him we are freed from the power of sin and reconciled to God. . . .

**Q:** What is the Holy Eucharist?

**A:** The Holy Eucharist is the sacrament commanded by Christ for the continual remembrance of his life, death, and resurrection, until his coming again.

**Q:** Why is the Eucharist called a sacrifice?

**A:** Because the Eucharist, the Church's sacrifice of praise and thanksgiving, is the way by which the sacrifice of Christ is made present, and in which he unites us to his one offering of himself.[4]"

### Comments

This week brings us to a frequently contested issue of Christian belief. Why did Jesus have to die? Why was his sacrifice necessary? What did his death actually "do" for you and me? While there are many, many different viewpoints in trying to answer these questions, it helps us to remember that these weeks build on each other. In Week One, we saw the problem: sin and evil. In Week Two, we saw that God walks with us. In this week, those two areas converge. Good triumphs over evil, but—like everything else in this world—there is a cost. Real change requires real sacrifice. We need to keep that truth right in front of us, and the Eucharist reminds us every week.

### Day 1: Examination

Read Matthew 26:20–46.

Ponder: What would be going through your mind if you were one of the disciples at the Last Supper? In the garden?

[Conversations with Christ on this topic]

### Day 2: Examination

Read Mark 14:43–52.

---

4. "An Outline of the Faith," in the Book of Common Prayer, 850, 859.

Ponder: In the space of ten verses, the disciples' entire world fell apart. What did they feel as they "fled"? What would you do?

[Conversations with Christ on this topic]

### Day 3: Examination

Read Luke 22:66–71.

Ponder: These were the religious leaders. They should have known better. Think on a time that you "should have known better." Why did you go against your better nature? How did that choice turn out?

[Conversations with Christ on this topic]

### Day 4: Examination

Read Luke 23:6–12.

Ponder: What happens when no one takes responsibility? Have you "passed the buck" recently? What might you have done differently?

[Conversations with Christ on this topic]

### Day 5: Examination

Read 1 Peter 4:12–5:11.

Ponder: How are our own sacrifices connected to Christ's sacrifice?

[Conversations with Christ on this topic]

## Ending Thought on Sacrifice and Eucharist

To sum up, Jesus on the Cross is both the symbol and the reality of the immense labour of the centuries which has, little by little, raised up the created spirit and brought it back to the depths of the divine milieu [i.e., the Kingdom of God]. He represents (and in a true sense, he is) creation, as, upheld by God, it re-ascends the slopes of being, sometimes clinging to things for support, sometimes tearing itself from them in order to pass beyond them, and always compensating, by physical suffering, for the setbacks caused by its moral downfalls. —Pierre Teilhard de Chardin[5]

Ponder: What does the Cross mean to you?

---

5. Pierre Teilhard de Chardin, *The Divine Milieu* (New York: Harper & Row, 1968), 104.

## Potential Journaling Prompts/Discussion Questions on Sacrifice and Eucharist

1. Do you see in your own life how the value system of Christ operates?
2. Can you see this value system operative in the social structures of your city, country, church? How do you react?
3. Do you want to live with less fear? Can you ask Jesus for help to become more like him?
4. Have you experienced the difficulty of sharing a loved one's pain?
5. What would you do differently if it were your last week on earth?

## Theme of the Fourth Week: Resurrection

"**Q:** What is the significance of Jesus' resurrection?

**A:** By his resurrection, Jesus overcame death and opened for us the way of eternal life. . . .

**Q:** What do we mean when we say that he ascended into heaven and is seated at the right hand of the Father?

**A:** We mean that Jesus took our human nature into heaven where he now reigns with the Father and intercedes for us.

**Q:** How can we share in his victory over sin, suffering, and death?

**A:** We share in his victory when we are baptized into the New Covenant and become living members of Christ.⁶"

### Comments

Resurrection is the heart of the Christian faith. There have been many prophets, teachers, sages, and reformers in the history of the world. Many good men and women have died for what they believed would change the world. Only one came back. The Gospels are his story, and we are his story too, if we will believe.

### Day 1: Examination

Read Mark 16:1–11.

---

6. "An Outline of the Faith," in the Book of Common Prayer, 850.

Ponder: Why did Jesus appear first to Mary Magdalene?

[Conversations with Christ on this topic]

### Day 2: Examination

Read Luke 24:13–35.

Ponder: Have you ever felt your heart "burning" within you about something? Why? Also, put yourself in the disciples' shoes; what do you suppose it was like to have Jesus "open" the scriptures to them?

[Conversations with Christ on this topic]

### Day 3: Examination

Read John 20:19–29.

Ponder: How might you react in Thomas' place? Is doubt always a bad thing? Also, ponder that Thomas is the first person to refer to Jesus as "God."

[Conversations with Christ on this topic]

### Day 4: Examination

Read John 21:1–17.

Ponder: What was going through the mind of Peter as Jesus asked him to "Feed my sheep"? Bear in mind that Peter's statement of "I am going fishing" at the beginning of the passage actually means: "I am going back to fishing as a profession." Does that put this conversation in a new light?

[Conversations with Christ on this topic]

### Day 5: Examination

Read Matthew 28:16–20 and Acts 1:1–11.

Ponder: These last two passages are written as much to us as they were to the disciples. What will you do now? How will you honor Christ's final words?

[Conversations with Christ on this topic]

## Ending Thought on Resurrection

If you want to identify me ask me not where I live, or what I like to eat, or how I comb my hair, but ask me what I am living for, in detail, and ask me what I think is keeping me from living fully for the things I want to live for. Between those two answers you can determine the identity of any person.[7] —Thomas Merton

Ponder: What do you live for? What is keeping you from fully living for that?

### Potential Journaling Prompts
### or Discussion Questions on Resurrection

1. Have you experienced the presence of the risen Jesus?
2. What gives you your greatest happiness?
3. Have you had any experiences of God's creative presence in your life? How did you feel?
4. Would you want to be more aware of God's presence in your everyday life?
5. What might keep you from desiring an awareness of God's presence?

## COMMON QUESTIONS

**Q:** Do I have to do all four weeks?

**A:** No, I have set the themes up in four weeks to follow Ignatius' original model. Feel free to pick a specific week or two that deals with the themes that are impacting you at the time.

**Q:** Is it necessary to look at the themes in the order you suggest?

**A:** Always feel free to adapt the format of a practice to fit you, but the order of the themes is intentional. These themes build on each other. We begin right where we are—in the middle of struggles, mistakes, and imperfections (i.e., sin). From that point, we can see that Jesus entered into that type of life willingly and showed what it could be like (i.e., incarnation). The themes of sacrifice and Eucharist show how Christ addressed the problems of the world and how he invites people to participate in the solution with him are third. Finally, the theme of resurrection is the ultimate end of the Christian story, so it fits as the theme at the end of the weeks. Resurrection is the hope for each person and for the entire creation in Christian terms.

---

7. Thomas Merton, *My Argument with the Gestapo* (New York: New Directions, 1975), 160–61.

Q: What if I only like one of the practices, either the Examination or Conversations with Christ?

A: By all means, use the one that resonates with you most; however, I advise you not to be too quick to dismiss the other practice. Remember, these practices are intended to bring us to an uncomfortable place. It's never easy to face our own shortcomings, so if you want to omit a practice on the basis of it being uncomfortable, then you might be missing the point of the spiritual exercises of St. Ignatius.

Q: Why is sin so important to this practice?

A: While sin is a prominent feature in most Christian understandings of history and the present state of the world, sin is particularly significant in Ignatian spirituality, and in Jesuit theology more generally. From this perspective, sin is the ultimate barrier that keeps humanity away from God. It must be dealt with again and again in order to move forward in knowing God.

Q: Is journaling more essential to this practice than others?

A: I have included many journaling prompts as a means to record and externalize your internal thought processes as you go through these meditations. They are not the only means for doing so. In fact, traditional Ignatian exercises use the sacrament of confession for this purpose rather than journaling. Yet, whether through speaking or writing, it is important to work through these themes by putting your thoughts into words.

Q: How often should I practice these Ignatian exercises?

A: Members of the Jesuit order go through a contemplative retreat based on these exercises at least once a year. These spiritual exercises are ideally suited for an annual check of your progress on the spiritual journey. Still, feel free to experiment. Find what works best for you.

# 5

## Reframing

### BRIEF BACKGROUND

As we go through our day-to-day lives, we often meet frustration, disappointment, hostility, and all manner of negativity. These feelings may come to us from others, or they might bubble up from within. It helps to have a way to acknowledge these feelings—not just ignore or deny them—and move to a more positive place, a place of gratitude. This practice is not historically limited to spirituality or religion, but it is an interesting possibility for deepening our spiritual lives because a large part of spirituality is the process of learning to see with new eyes. This practice offers some practical tips to implement a new perspective.

### HOW TO PRACTICE

You can follow these steps by speaking aloud or by simply thinking through the method:

1. Identify the feeling(s) you have. Be as specific as possible. After all, there might be a gulf of difference for you between anger and annoyance or disappointment and frustration.
2. If necessary, identify the cause of that feeling(s). The cause may be external or internal. Also, there may be multiple causes. Identify all possible causes.
3. Take five deep breaths.
4. Mentally, imagine setting aside that feeling. You're not forgetting, ignoring, or minimizing your feeling. You are simply setting it aside for now.
5. Think about the good things happening in your life. Name at least one good happening. It can be large or small. There is no need to find something comparable or analogous to your negative feeling.

6. Now, give that good happening the same treatment that you did for the negative one. Identify the feeling(s) surrounding that happening. Be as specific as possible.

7. Go ahead and identify the cause(s). This step may be particularly difficult. It is often much easier to identify negative causes because we want to assign blame. Positive causes are often more overlooked. We often have to learn to be grateful.

8. If you can identify a person as a cause for a good happening in your life, then go and find them. Thank them verbally, in person if possible. If you cannot identify a particular person as a cause, then go and find someone (probably someone you already know) and tell them about the good thing that has happened to you and that you are grateful for it.

9. Repeat the process for each negative feeling or happening that seems to be plaguing your thoughts.

## VARIATIONS

Try these additional versions:

### Writing

If you are not as comfortable speaking as writing, or just want a change, then try going through the method by writing everything out rather than speaking it. When you get to the steps that require contacting others, simply write them a letter, an e-mail, or social media message.

### Habit

Reframing is a great practice to work into a habit. The most successful method for making a habit out of reframing is to do it at regular intervals. For instance, you can go through the negative and positive feelings steps at mealtimes. You can then look for moments in the day at work, school, or home to communicate those feelings to others.

### Group

Reframing is a particularly effective practice to use in a group setting. Hearing the emotions that others mention will often remind you of certain feelings that you also have. Having several persons in a group may also help to jog your own memory about good things happening to you for which you can be grateful. Most importantly, you have a built-in step of sharing your positive feelings and good happenings with other people right then and there.

## COMMON QUESTIONS

**Q:** Why identify the feeling first and then the cause? Isn't that a bit backward?

**A:** I have reversed their order on purpose because I find it easy to jump to whom or what I blame for a feeling. The harder part is to acknowledge that, one way or the other, I am the one having the feeling, so it is ultimately my responsibility. The reversed order helps me to remember that I am rarely an innocent bystander in the process of getting my feelings hurt.

**Q:** What if you are not sure if something is part of the cause or not?

**A:** Include it anyway. For instance, if I am frustrated with a particular project at work, one cause I may include is whether I feel physically tired, even on days that I would never admit to anything being my fault.

**Q:** What if I can't fully distinguish each feeling or among feelings?

**A:** Try your best to be specific, but sometimes feelings just get mixed up. Say how you're feeling as best you can, however you can. No one is keeping score on how well you distinguish your feelings. This process is for you.

**Q:** Is it so important to find something or someone good? Could I just focus on putting the negative feelings into perspective?

**A:** It really is essential to find something good. You don't need to worry about finding a good thing that specifically "cancels out" the bad. You will rarely have such closely comparable good and bad happenings, and the funny thing is that we never seem to value them similarly. Sometimes, the good shines out and overshadows the bad. At other times, negative feelings seemingly cast a pall on even the best things we have going in our lives. The point is that you are deliberately holding before your mind something good and being grateful for it. Our ways of thinking are formed by many influences, but one of the single, greatest influences on our mental patterns is the process of repetition. If we repeatedly keep gratefulness actively on our mind, it is far more effective than just trying not to think pessimistically.

**Q:** Do I have to go and tell others about the good thing?

**A:** While I would love to make this step voluntary—because I definitely belong to the introvert tribe, some might even call me "king"—there is a deep effectiveness to our gratefulness when we communicate it to others. I am not advocating insincerity. Only share what you are authentically grateful for, but share. For us introverts, I've included the possibility of sharing through writing. That variation takes away some of the potential anxiety.

**Q:** Does this practice ask someone in pain to accept that pain in a fatalistic way?

**A:** This is a very important issue. No, this practice is not intended to encourage fatalism. Reframing helps us to see the good that is present in our lives, not to accept the bad and start calling it "good." If you can change your circumstances—can do something about your pain—then do it. Reframing is a spiritual practice to embolden us to live fully.

**Q:** What if I still feel upset?

**A:** That's perfectly normal. After all, you're human. You are more than capable of feeling two things at once. The point is now you are not only feeling upset. You've reminded yourself that even in the midst of disappointment gratefulness can exist, and where gratefulness can exist so can hope.

## POTENTIAL JOURNALING PROMPTS OR DISCUSSION QUESTIONS

1. How do you define gratitude or appreciation?
2. How do you feel when confronted with disappointment? What about your most recent disappointment?
3. How do you feel when you are grateful for someone or something? What do you feel in your mind, body, and emotions?
4. What feelings are hardest for you to feel at the same time?
5. What would change in your life if you practiced reframing as a habit?
6. What are some ways that we are all connected with each other?

# 6

## Observing

### BRIEF BACKGROUND

As you have probably gathered by this point, the practices in this section are principally about learning to focus on the present—right here, right now. To build this sense of presence, there are many practices that help us learn to pay attention. Often, the hardest task in paying attention is to learn to pay attention to our senses, which are constantly giving us information. For instance, we are so familiar with the sense of sight that we often gloss over the miracle of it, and we miss the chance for deeper attention to what we see. The practice of observing helps us to slow down and focus on what we see both in the details and in the big picture.

### HOW TO PRACTICE

This practice is based on a very old proverb, The Blind Men and the Elephant:

1. Imagine that you were asked to touch one part of an elephant with your eyes closed. How would you describe each part?
2. If you only touched the side of the elephant, how would you describe an elephant?
3. If you only touched the tusk of the elephant, how would you describe an elephant?
4. If you only touched the trunk of the elephant, how would you describe an elephant?
5. If you only touched the knee of the elephant, how would you describe an elephant?
6. If you only touched the ear of the elephant, how would you describe an elephant?

7. If you only touched the tail of the elephant, how would you describe an elephant?

While this practice might seem a bit too obvious or silly, we often make similar mistakes because we see but do not pay enough attention to observe. Through the practice of observing, we learn to step back mindfully to hold both the fine details and the big picture in our attention.

## VARIATIONS

There are as many variations to this exercise as potential subject matter that we can observe. Ideally, we bring this sense of observation into our everyday lives to see anew. However, here are a couple of variations you might want to try as a discrete practice:

### Duck or Rabbit

There is a psychology test first used by Joseph Jastrow in which one may see either a rabbit or duck. Which do you see first? Can you see the other? You might want to ponder how difficult it is to see both duck and rabbit simultaneously. What might that insight have to say about difficulties of observation?

### Children's Book

Find a children's book without words or one in which you can easily cover up or ignore the words. If possible, use a book for which you do not know the story. Look, really look, at each picture. What do you observe? What do you imagine the story to be from the images alone? If you have covered up the words, then uncover them and compare your story with what is written. How similar or different are the two stories? Common wisdom tells us that a picture is worth a thousand words, but this is only true if we take the time to observe. You can also expand this variation to include other pieces of artwork.

## COMMON QUESTIONS

**Q:** Does one observation have to be right and all others wrong? Is there really only one right way to see the elephant? Is there actually a duck or a rabbit?

A: One of the most important outcomes of this exercise is practice in non-dualistic thinking. When we think in dualistic terms, we think in terms of either-or. Either it really is a duck or it really is a rabbit. Nondualistic thinking tries to hold attention in the space of both-and. Perhaps it is both a duck and a rabbit. Perhaps all the observations of the elephant are true simultaneously.

Q: Is the sense of sight the only sense that I can use in this practice?

A: Absolutely not. You can use all five senses—or any other senses you possess—in this manner. I chose sight because it is the easiest to describe. However, we can stop and pay attention with any of our senses rather than just go through life with them set on "automatic." If you like this practice, challenge yourself with learning to be observant with hearing, touch, and the other senses as well.

Q: How do I move from using this practice to observing in everyday life?

A: The key to the answer is found in the question itself: practice. As you practice observing, you'll begin to catch yourself in the act of bringing that sense of attention to your normal life. I recommend letting this crossover develop naturally rather than setting specific goals for the practice of observing in your everyday activities. It is easy to go overboard if you are relentless in maintaining observation before you have built it up as a habit and practice. Go easy on yourself. Be patient.

Q: What about seeing beneath the surface or "reading between the lines" of everyday life?

A: This is a very natural question in the progression of practicing observing, but it does tend to jump ahead. I include it here because it was a question that tripped me up a lot when I first began mindfulness practices. The difficult answer is that the practice of observing is about slowing us down from jumping to the "inner meaning" of things too quickly. Often, a diligent, measured observation of the surface of things—of life—yield important, though subtle, insights that we would completely miss if we jump too quickly into looking for hidden meanings and inner truth.

Q: What do I do if the big picture and the details don't seem to match up?

A: Then don't rush too quickly into trying to harmonize those differences. Stay in that moment of tension where things don't match up. You may find that you are seeing reality more clearly when you stay in paradox. After all, what's really more important—making sense of reality or seeing reality for what it actually is?

**Q:** How does this practice connect with seeing with "spiritual eyes"?

**A:** One of the clearest indicators is that you begin to see people a little differently. This new perspective is exactly what is illustrated beautifully in the prayer of St. Patrick (see chapter 10).

## POTENTIAL JOURNALING PROMPTS OR DISCUSSION QUESTIONS

1. What positive experiences did you have while practicing this practice?
2. What negative experiences did you have while practicing this practice?
3. How did you adapt this structure to your situation? Were there any new images you added?
4. What could be the day-to-day benefits of learning to observe?
5. What did you find most difficult in this practice? How? Why?
6. Did any unexpected insights arise while you practiced? What were they?

# 7

## Journaling

### BRIEF BACKGROUND

As you may have noticed, I include journaling prompts with every chapter, so that should be a clue as to the potential applicability of journaling as a spiritual practice. As for background, the origin of journaling is lost in the dim mists of prehistory, but the appeal for writing down one's thoughts and experiences with a spiritual intention is widespread. At least since St. Augustine's *Confessions*, the practice of writing down one's experiences has played a continuing role within Christian spirituality. However, the role of a journal is not the proprietary property of one religion or even religion in general. Many autobiographies begin as journals from individuals that do not adhere to any predetermined religious purpose for their writing or deeply held beliefs of their own. For instance, Henry David Thoreau's *On Walden Pond* (or simply Walden) is an intensely spiritual work that does not typically appeal to traditional religious sensibilities. Suffice it to say, the history of journaling is so broad that this practice is what you make of it, and the ways it can help you spiritually and psychologically to write about your experiences and reflect on their meaning.

### HOW TO PRACTICE

I'm afraid that I might be starting to sound like a broken record in reiterating the choice is yours on how to use journaling in your spiritual life, but for the sake of having somewhere to start, let me offer a few guidelines.

1. To begin, you may want to make a few logistical decisions. Are you going to put pen to paper? Would you rather type up your thoughts? Are you going to strive to make this practice a daily one, at least while you're trying it out? What time of day would you prefer to journal? Are

you going to journal for a certain length of time or a certain number of pages? These and other "set up" factors can make the difference between journaling once and giving the practice a sincere attempt in order to assess the impact it makes on your life.

2. The next step is to think about what your approach to your own experiences is: analytical, practical, experiential, reflective, conceptual, potential, relational, or emotional. While you can easily combine approaches in a mix-and-match style, it is often helpful to start off from one particular frame of reference. Let me offer some potential questions to illustrate my meaning.

3. For the analytical person, try journaling about an important problem for you at home or work. How have you tried to solve it in the past? What approaches or methods would you like to try? For the practical person, try journaling about a way to organize some part of your life that you want to change. What are the actual steps to realizing your goal? For the experiential person, journal about your experiences for that day. Where in your day did you feel most alive and in the present moment? For the reflective person, what memory came up in your life today? What triggered it? How is that memory connected for good or bad to your own personal story? For the conceptual person, journal about what you would change about your life, family, workplace, or world. What is your vision and how could you follow it in reality tomorrow? For the potential person, what ideas did you come across today? What possibilities does the future hold? What kind of person would you like to be tomorrow? For the relational person, you might journal about someone close to you. What would you like to do to build that relationship? How would you like for that other person to succeed? For the emotional person, try journaling on a major feeling you had today. What situation or person instigated that feeling? Can you assign a color to that feeling? How can that feeling teach you and help you to grow as a person?

4. If journaling by approach seems a little too abstract, you can always start by journaling through your five senses. Choose an event that happened in your day. For instance, what did you do when you first woke up? Then go through all five senses to ground yourself in that remembrance. When you first awoke, what did you see, hear, smell, taste, or touch?

5. As you journal, if you are seeking to approach the practice in a spiritual manner, try to keep a few questions in the frame of that aspect of life: how did such-and-such event impact your relationship with God, what could today tell you about the illusory (or transient) nature of life, what does your life mean, where is the universe going, what meaning lies behind the basic facts of everyday living?

# VARIATIONS

While many obvious variations exist according to subject or approach, there are a few less obvious variations that you might want to consider.

## Format

You may think of doing a video journal. Also, many creative individuals prefer to journal through a series of drawings or paintings. How about poetry or song? Perhaps you would like to write a play. You also could write a blog that incorporates elements of journaling.

## Movement

While journaling is typically attached to writing, you could create a dance or routine movement that you can associate with a particular memory, feeling, or idea.

## Reading

Reading the journals and spiritual autobiographies of others will not only give you some interesting ideas for how to approach your own journaling, but also give you some insight into the characters and experiences of potential spiritual role models.

## Sharing

It is easy to assume that journaling is an entirely solitary activity, but you can easily adapt journaling to the spiritual connections and relationships of sharing with a good friend or intimate partner. Journaling can also be the basis of group work of all types, ranging from therapeutic goals to aims of refining writing ability.

# COMMON QUESTIONS

**Q:** What do I do when I don't know what to write?

**A:** It's important to remember that this practice is by no means mandatory, so don't force yourself to write just because you feel that you should. Still, if you are trying to set up a regular practice, then it might be difficult to know where to begin. In that case, you might try some free-writing. Give yourself three to five minutes to write anything that comes to mind. You don't need to write in complete sentences, have good spelling, or even be coherent. Just put words on the page. This practice can often loosen you up, and I typically find that I "come around" to what I really want to journal about as I go through this prewriting process.

**Q:** Could journaling be viewed as a type of prayer?

**A:** Absolutely. I view most of my journals as a type of prayer. You can even address particular entries to God, if you so desire.

**Q:** Should I keep my journals?

**A:** The answer really depends on you. If you want to keep your journals, then keep them. If you don't, then toss them. I've instructed my wife to burn mine in the case of any mysterious circumstances surrounding my death (just kidding). Seriously, these journals are just for you so you can do whatever you want with them.

**Q:** How is journaling different from thinking deeply about my experience?

**A:** That's a more important question than it seems. There is some indefinable quality about the process of writing your thoughts down that begins the process of synthesis and reflection. Whether you feel it or not, writing your thoughts down begins the process of making sense of your life experiences. In that sense, journaling is an invaluable tool even if you only use it infrequently.

**Q:** Should I share my journals?

**A:** Again, that's entirely up to you. In my experience, I have chosen not to share my journals. I like the freedom of writing whatever I feel in whatever terms I want without even the slightest thought to communicating my thoughts coherently to others. However, I do occasionally pull events from journal entries for speaking occasions or for other types of writing. If I do so, I completely rewrite the event, experience, or reflection so that it will communicate to an audience. Yet, I would likely never have the reflections on the meaning of my experiences without first journaling about them.

**Q:** Can journaling be combined with other spiritual practices?

**A:** Yes, journaling pairs well with many different spiritual practices. For instance, you can journal about your insights from *lectio divina* or various mindfulness practices. The only caveat is that some practices do not lend themselves well to include journaling during the specific act of the practice. For instance, journaling during a centering prayer session (see chapter 8) would lead to a defeating level of distraction. In these cases, you might journal before or after you engage in a particular spiritual practice.

**Q:** Should I write in first person, second person, or third person?

**A:** While you can experiment with personal preferences here, I recommend journaling in the first person as your default setting. Most of us think in first person ("I, me, my"), so it is an easier transition. Writing in second or third person tends to set up a distance between our interpretations and the events themselves. You might save second or third person for the type of reflective journaling that seeks to separate out the exact facts of your experience from your feelings and interpretations of how an experience made you feel.

**Q:** How much should I worry about accuracy in my journaling?

**A:** Don't care a bit. Your journal is for you, so make it as accurate as you like. Still, you might want to make sure to write legibly enough that your future self could still read it. Aside from that, go wild.

**Q:** What if my journaling just seems to be repetitive?

**A:** You may not be bringing a reflective eye to your writing. Try to write more about the meaning of what happened rather than the simple facts of what happened. If you find that you are stuck journaling about a certain thought, event, or feeling, that circumstance might be a clue that you are obsessing over some part of your experience. I recommend consulting with a therapist or priest at this point because there may be deeper issues brewing under the surface. Conversely, you can sometimes "unstick" yourself from repetitive journaling by writing about the reasons you think led to you becoming stuck. At least, that's a new angle on your old topic.

Q: What if my journaling becomes just a lot of "ranting"?

A: Don't worry too much about ranting. A journal is often the perfect place to vent these feelings. However, if you find that your journal is just one rant after another, you might start exploring where all the anger is originating. This circumstance is another good potential opportunity for consulting with a therapist, counselor, or clergyperson.

## POTENTIAL JOURNALING PROMPTS OR DISCUSSION QUESTIONS

1. What positive experiences did you have while practicing this practice? (Journaling about journaling might seem a little too reductive, but you might give it a try anyway.)
2. What negative experiences did you have while practicing this practice?
3. How did you adapt this structure to your situation?
4. How did you meet God in this practice?
5. How did journaling change your perspective spiritually or just your perspective on the usefulness of journaling?
6. What about journaling surprised you?

# Section 2

---

## LISTENING

### WHAT IS CONTEMPLATION?

Most of the time, when you run into the word *contemplation*, it means something along the lines of thinking deeply, as if it were a synonym for the word *concentration*. It is perfectly fine to use the word in that sense, but that is not what I mean by it here.

The term *contemplative prayer* was coined to denote all of the disciplines, techniques, and practices in prayer that focus upon listening to God rather than talking at him. Contemplation "proper" is the moment—completely out of the control of the individual person—when God self-reveals in some way to you. As I briefly mentioned in chapter 3 while considering the steps of *lectio divina*, it could be through a voice, dream, or vision—but, perhaps more often, it could be as simple as an insight or memory. Still, contemplation is where the excitement is. Contemplation is the moment when God communicates with an individual, whether it is through words, images, or any other medium. It might be through a burning bush, a descending dove, or even something as simple as the words of a trusted friend—but God is there!

Have you ever had such a moment?

What would you do if contemplation ever happened to you?

Trying to answer that second question is where the practices of this section have their place. Simply stated, these practices are designed to quiet our minds before God, especially when it seems so impossible to keep ourselves from running after every type of distraction. We cannot control contemplation, but we can learn how to listen more effectively. However, that's only the work of preparation for the moment of contemplation. These practices will also be valuable to you during contemplation for recognizing those often subtle moments for what they are; they can help you after the moment of contemplation when you need to reflect on what has just happened in order to decide how to respond. Within my own experience, I have discovered that without a framework to reflect fruitfully on the contemplative moment, it is all too tempting to just set up camp in that moment and have "warm, fuzzy feelings" about it without any real change in our lives. So with these definitions and purposes in mind, let's take a look at the practices of listening: centering prayer, clarity, loving-kindness reflection, and letting go.

# 8

## Centering Prayer

### BRIEF BACKGROUND

Thomas Keating and M. Basil Pennington were the first to define centering prayer; however, they noted points of contact between this prayer method, Thomas Merton, and the historic practice of contemplative prayer. In the 1970s and 1980s they offered it as both a gateway toward contemplative prayer and as an alternative to the then-popular practice of transcendental meditation. While contemplative prayer has been practiced for millennia in Christian monasteries and convents, it was typically taught only as a total lifestyle commitment. Centering prayer offers a simple method to enter into the contemplative silences that are at the heart of Christian monasticism. In the practice of centering prayer, you ideally section off two twenty-minute periods of time a day to pray. In that time, you sit quietly, not attempting to speak or ask God anything; rather, use a simple word such as *God* or *love* to focus yourself whenever your mind begins to wander.

### HOW TO PRACTICE

1. Choose a word that is personally meaningful to you as a reminder to seek God within. In other words, choose a single word or short phrase to remind yourself of God whenever you realize that your mind has wandered off during prayer. Try not to change the word too often, especially during the prayer time. You can use practically any word, including *God, love, hope, mercy,* or *mystery.*

2. Next, sit comfortably with your eyes closed. Breathe slowly in and out of your nose for a minute or two to settle yourself down. You could also pray a short introductory prayer, such as "For God alone my soul waits in silence, for my hope is from him" (Ps. 62:5). Then quietly introduce the word you have chosen to remind you of God.

51

3. Continue sitting silently for twenty minutes, listening to the silence. When thoughts begin to arise, just repeat your word aloud or think it silently.

4. At the end of the prayer period, remain in silence with eyes closed for a few moments. Reciting the Lord's Prayer slowly is a good way to return your thoughts to the world around you. You might also want to get up and walk around for a few moments rather than immediately beginning a new task in order to reorient yourself.

5. As you are practicing this prayer, keep these practical points in mind:

   - The recommended time for this prayer is twenty minutes. Keating and Pennington suggest two periods each day: one first thing in the morning and the other in the afternoon or early evening. However, don't let time be what stops you. If you can only do five minutes, then do five minutes. On the other hand, you might find the practice so valuable, or your thoughts so hard to tame, that you want to spend longer.

   - The end of the prayer period can be signaled by an alarm. A relatively quiet alarm is helpful not to jar you out of the prayer time.

   - Unlike many forms of meditation, the goal of centering prayer is not particularly about being as still as possible. If you need to shift your position or scratch an itch, do so. Just try not to make a habit of fidgeting. Also, as you pray, you might become more aware of your body sensations. While that awareness can be interesting, it is not the goal of the practice. Simply note your observation and then proceed back to your word.

   - The effects of centering prayer occur most noticeably outside of the prayer time, but they are subtle results—increasing calmness, patience, an inner stillness. Don't try to make your prayer time perfect. Just try to be consistent. God sees your effort and loves you for it.

## VARIATIONS

Usually your prayer word is an excellent way to nudge your attention back when your mind wanders. However, you might also like to try these variations to see how they strike you:

## With Breath

Some of the earliest Christian mystics synchronized their prayers with their own breathing. Theologically speaking, such a practice is not that far-fetched. After all, both Hebrew and Greek use the same word for breath and spirit. Try counting to five as you breathe in, and counting to five as you breathe out. Slowly. Calmly. Attentively.

## With Music

Obviously, music is an area where individual tastes vary widely. Experiment. Find out what works for you. I have had the most success with quiet, wordless music playing in the background. When centering, I have found that I get caught up in lyrics if I use music with words. On the other hand, you might try using Gregorian chants. I also love using the sounds of nature (e.g., rushing wind, calling birds, waterfalls). You can find free recordings of these types of sounds all over the Internet, or you might try centering outside, provided you have a relatively secluded place to pray.

## With Candles

Most variations of a centering prayer practice have the participants close their eyes in order to focus inwardly in a more effective manner. However, some of us might have even more difficulty concentrating with our eyes closed. If you find yourself included in this number, then try to center in a dark room with a single candle for illumination. Focus on the flame. When I practice centering prayer in this way, I also use the phrase *Awaken hope* as a sacred word to center. These words come from one of the evening prayers from the Book of Common Prayer, which states:

> Lord Jesus, stay with us, for evening is at hand and the day is past; be our companion in the way, kindle our hearts and awaken hope, that we may know you as you are revealed in Scripture and the breaking of bread. Grant this for the sake of your love. Amen.[1]

Center your gaze, and see if your spirit will follow.

---

1. Book of Common Prayer, 124.

## With an Image

If your prayer word does not seem to be helping today, or any day, and/or you're a very visually focused person, then try to get your imagination to work for you rather than against you. For instance, visualize your flow of thoughts as a swiftly moving stream. Then imagine yourself wading into them. Stand there for a moment, then begin to sink beneath the surface. In your mind's eye, continue sinking until you reach the bottom. Now the constant stream of your thoughts is flowing overhead, but you are on the bottom of the river bed where it is dark and still. Lock a heavy weight on to your ankle to keep you down there, and imagine that the weight is shaped as your prayer word. Each time you feel a "tug" to the "surface," that weight keeps you anchored. At the end of the prayer time, you can unlock the weight and float to the surface. You might also want to use a simple image rather than an entire scenario. That's fine too. If you are interested in using an external image, then you might skip down to chapter 17 on praying with icons and incorporate some steps from that practice into how you do centering prayer.

## COMMON QUESTIONS

**Q:** What if I've never done any type of contemplative or meditative practice before?

**A:** First of all, go easy on yourself. Don't expect too much out of the practice until you get used to the "mechanics" of it. Additionally, be aware that you may have thoughts, feelings, or memories surface that are particularly troubling. This circumstance is very common for persons with post-traumatic stress disorder (PTSD) or complex post-traumatic stress disorder (CPTSD). If this circumstance happens to you, please consult with a mental health professional. If you do not know a mental health professional, your local priest, pastor, or spiritual leader can recommend one to you.

**Q:** Does the prayer word have to be only one word?

**A:** No, it can be two or three words. However, it is best to keep it short. You are using that word to draw your attention away from stray thoughts. You aren't trying to start a new train of thought.

**Q:** How often should I repeat the prayer word?

A: It varies widely with each participant; however, remember that your prayer word is not a mantra. You are not repeating it unceasingly to drive out thought. Thoughts will come and go. Let them. The word is only a reminder for you when you have drawn a stray thought back to consider.

Q: What if I keep thinking about something I can't get out of my mind?

A: Don't be too hard on yourself. This happens to everyone. God sees your effort and realizes that some prayer times are harder than others. If you are particularly agitated or anxious through these obsessive thoughts, then just get up and go for a quiet walk and try again next time. No one is "keeping score."

Q: What if I spend the whole time "fighting" with my thoughts?

A: This "battle" happens from time to time with even the most experienced practitioner. Do not try to center "perfectly" because you will only find yourself frustrated. Don't take yourself too seriously. However, if it seems that "fighting" is all you do, then you might try one of the other practices suggested in these pages. Not every practice resonates with every person. Find the one(s) that fit you.

Q: What if I fall asleep?

A: This will very likely happen from time to time, especially at first. Don't worry. Maybe God sees you need some rest, and that is the "answer" to prayer that you need right now. However, if you seem to fall asleep every time, then you might try to center at different times of the day or in different positions. If I am particularly tired, I like to sit on the floor while I pray. It is slightly uncomfortable for me, and that's just enough to keep me from getting sleepy. Still, don't be too hard on yourself; don't make yourself too uncomfortable. Experiment until you find what might be that "slightly uncomfortable" spot for you.

Q: What if I have an insight, experience, or vision during centering prayer?

A: Thank God for it. However, try not to dwell on it too much, particularly during the prayer time. Mystical experiences are not the "goal" of centering prayer. Experiences are nice, but the main aim of centering prayer is a lifestyle that is more quietly focused on God and being open to the spiritual in everyday life. It's a subtle, calming effect, but you'll see it happen in your life over time—and those around you will notice it far more than you do.

**Q:** What if I don't experience a sense of stillness or peace during centering prayer?

**A:** Don't worry. Sometimes you may feel a sense of peace or quiet; often you won't. In centering prayer, you are training yourself to be open and listening to God. That state of being is not necessarily connected to a particular feeling. Let the feelings come and go as they please.

**Q:** What if I don't feel like I'm doing anything?

**A:** I guarantee that you'll feel this way part of the time. It feels so alien in our fast-paced culture to take time out to do nothing—and to actually do nothing. See if you can settle into a state of attentive waiting on God, and, perhaps, make a note of how surprising it is that simple boredom can make you so uncomfortable.

## POTENTIAL JOURNALING PROMPTS OR DISCUSSION QUESTIONS

1. What positive experiences did you have while practicing this practice?
2. What negative experiences did you have while practicing this practice?
3. How did you adapt this structure to your situation?
4. How did you meet God in this practice?
5. How did silence help you listen to God?
6. What prayer word(s) did you use throughout the week, and how did it help you focus?
7. How aware have you become of the distractions both in prayer and in everyday life?

# 9

## Clarity

### BRIEF BACKGROUND

How can we listen when we're distracted? How can we listen when our inner voice is screaming too loudly? While all mindfulness practices can help us relax and re-center, sometimes we find ourselves especially stressed, anxious, distracted, or frenzied. More tangible and symbolic practices are particularly helpful when we are stressed. It may be difficult to focus on our own inner thoughts when everything seems spiraling out of control, so let's give our minds a little help through externalizing our inner turmoil. Let's seek some clarity.

### HOW TO PRACTICE

You will need a snow globe or a similar object to use this practice:

1. Hold the snow globe in your hand stretched out from your body at shoulder level. See the clarity of the water. It is easy to see through the water to the other side.
2. Shake the ball. Watch the "snow" whirl and swirl, catching the light. See how clouded the water in the globe becomes.
3. Put your other hand on your stomach. Feel the rise and fall of your breathing. Take five deep breaths here, as you watch the snow settle in the globe.
4. Continue to wait and breathe until the snow completely settles, and the water becomes clear once more.
5. Ponder how the busyness of your mind can cause whirling, swirling, and clouding just like the snow globe.
6. Feel free to repeat the process.

## VARIATIONS

While some later practices function as variations of this practice, I find it difficult to think of a suitable replacement for the snow globe here. If you can think of other items that work similarly, then try them out. Stretch yourself. Finding a symbolic object that is particularly meaningful to you will greatly enhance the effectiveness of this practice. I also suggest experimenting with music in this practice, particularly if you have access to a piece of music that begins loud and dissonant but gradually becomes quiet and harmonious.

## COMMON QUESTIONS

**Q:** What if these last few "symbolic" practices aren't meaningful to me?

**A:** Like with all of these practices, if you don't find one or more particularly meaningful, then just move on to something else. As I've said previously, this is a sourcebook. Not all practices will appeal to everyone. Honestly, several practices only appeal to me under certain circumstances. However, if you sense that you have a deeper issue with how symbolism enters into your spirituality, then it might be worthwhile to ponder what is bothering you because you will have a hard time finding spiritual practices that don't incorporate symbolism to one degree or another. Allow your pondering to run its course, which may well include consulting with a member of the clergy or a mental health professional.

**Q:** Is an object really necessary for this practice?

**A:** While I will stop short of saying it is absolutely essential, it is the intent of the clarity practice. It is specifically designed for us when we need to visualize and externalize our feelings.

**Q:** What if I still can't settle down and feel stressed, anxious, or distracted?

**A:** Well, then, you're probably human. This practice is meant to be an aid in settling down, but you might need to practice it quite a few times to notice any difference. Don't expect too much too soon out of the practice or yourself. If you have been in a constant state of motion, then it may take quite a while to remember how to settle down.

**Q:** What if I feel sped up after this practice?

**A:** This result may seem counterintuitive, but it happens fairly frequently. The practice is not actually speeding you up; rather, you are becoming more aware of what your body and mind have been trying to tell you. Actually, this feeling is an early indicator that this practice is effecting change in you. Peace will come, but sometimes we first have to realize just how out of sorts we actually are.

**Q:** Is it okay to combine this practice with the drumbeat practice (chapter 20)?

**A:** Sure. Give it a try. They combine particularly nicely when the clarity practice is placed at the end of the drumbeat practice. Think of it like a spiritual "cool-down."

**Q:** What if I can't ignore a particular image or thought in my head?

**A:** That's fine. You don't need to move away from that image or thought to practice clarity. It only becomes an issue if you are so distracted that you forget to see what's happening in the snow globe or to feel your own breathing. Remember that these practices are not about attaining a blank mind or getting rid of all thoughts. While certain forms of mindfulness do have detachment as a goal, none of the beginning practices in this book require that aim or mindset. Go easy on yourself. Let that mind just keep right on thinking; that's what it was designed for, after all.

## POTENTIAL JOURNALING PROMPTS OR DISCUSSION QUESTIONS

1. What positive experiences did you have while practicing this practice?
2. What negative experiences did you have while practicing this practice?
3. What do you feel in your body when you are stressed, anxious, and/or distracted?
4. What do you feel in your mind when you are stressed, anxious, and/or distracted?
5. What would it take for you to be able to think clearly?
6. Mindfulness practices are often coupled with other spiritual practices. What spiritual practices would you like to try combining with this mindful practice of clarity?

# 10

## Loving-Kindness Reflection

### BRIEF BACKGROUND

Many of these practices direct our attention to our own bodies and experience, but you may be interested in directing your focus elsewhere. That type of focused attention and intention can be directed outward as well—to family, friends, coworkers, and even the entire human race. If we intend to listen to God, then we must also prepare ourselves to listen to humanity—for God often speaks through the people who surround us. Loving-kindness reflection offers us a method to learn how to listen in this way. However—and this is a very important "however"—you cannot send out loving-kindness in a deep and meaningful way until you first can direct it toward yourself. I recommend spending several weeks or months with centering prayer (chapter 8) before moving to the practice of loving-kindness reflection, which is presented below. The following method was first articulated by Jon Kabat-Zinn in *Full Catastrophe Living*,[1] but I am adapting and simplifying it to an extent. You'll also notice that I connect it with Christian prayer, which Kabat-Zinn does not. So, with that said, let's give it a try . . .

### HOW TO PRACTICE

1. Begin by consciously focusing on your breath. Concentrate on your inhalation and exhalation for a count of ten. Also, you could focus for a few breaths on each of your five senses: sight, sound, smell, taste, and touch. What information are they giving to you in this moment?

---

1. Jon Kabat-Zinn, *Full Catastrophe Living: Using the Wisdom of Your Body and Mind to Face Stress, Pain, and Illness* (New York: Bantam Books, 2013), 214–17.

2. Gently close your eyes. Invite feelings of love, kindness, and peace to yourself. Draw up in your memory a time that you felt completely accepted by another person. If you cannot think of a specific instance, use your imagination or an example from history or fiction. As you breathe, focus on the feelings of that moment or event.

3. Say or think (to yourself), "I desire peace, happiness, and health for myself."

4. Try to draw up another person in your mind that you know. It helps to picture someone who is currently dealing with a difficult issue or problem. Initially, limit yourself to a single individual with whom you have personally met. You can branch out in later practice sessions.

5. With your next exhalation, imagine sending feelings of loving-kindness from yourself to that person. Say or think, "I desire peace, happiness, and health for _____."

6. You might feel like you are doing a whole lot of nothing, but remember that you are training your own attention. If you spend a few moments actually trying, then you have accomplished something real within yourself.

7. If you stick with this practice, you may want to branch out to multiple persons or even try a harder version of this practice—sending out loving-kindness to someone who has harmed you in some way. You may just find out that loving-kindness becomes forgiveness. However, if it does not, do not feel bad. You are still moving past the hurt feelings you have toward this person, breaking his/her hold over you. That's positive all by itself.

8. In the course of reflection, you may become aware of ways that you have harmed or slighted others. Send loving-kindness to them and forgiveness to yourself—and you may just feel the desire to ask them for forgiveness. If the circumstances reasonably allow, I would encourage you to follow this impulse. Loving-kindness is not just about abstract meditation; it is definitely an active practice too.

9. You can expand the scope of your reflection to include all of humanity, all living creatures, the planet, or the entire universe, but do not start there. Spend many sessions first with the small and specific. It's easy to lose focus and attention in the BIG; don't rush away from the beauty of the small.

10. Return to your own breathing for a few minutes before ending the reflection. Each session may last only five to ten minutes to be fruitful for you; however, you may want to expand that time greatly. Allow the time spent to ebb and flow as best fits you. There are no absolute rules for minimum or maximum length.

## VARIATIONS

While I feel that this practice speaks deeply to many different religious traditions, it can be combined with the well-known prayer of St. Patrick[2] for deep, deep value. As you breathe in and out, instead of speaking or thinking some variant of "I desire peace, happiness, and health for _____," pray one of the phrases of St. Patrick:

> Christ be with me, Christ before me,
> Christ be after me, Christ within me,
> Christ beneath me, Christ above me,
> Christ at my right hand, Christ at my left . . .
> Christ in the heart of every one who thinks of me,
> Christ in the mouth of every one who speaks to me.
> Christ in every eye that sees me.
> Christ in every ear that hears me.[3]

## COMMON QUESTIONS

**Q:** Why does the practice start with sending love to myself?

**A:** This is one of the most essential pieces of this practice. We often think that for love to be true that it is always directed outward, but we are incapable of offering more love and compassion than we are willing to direct toward ourselves. As counterintuitive as it may seem, the first step to compassion in reflection as well as action is to learn to be compassionate with yourself. The same reasoning is true for forgiveness.

**Q:** Are there any images for love, peace, or kindness that you recommend?

---

2. Music: "St. Patrick's Breastplate," *The Hymnal 1982* #370.

3. *The Catholic Prayer Book*, comp. Michael Buckley, ed. Tony Castle (Cincinnati: St. Anthony Messenger Press, 1986), 152.

A: Honestly, images for abstract, symbolic feelings vary so much from person to person. I envision an open hand, helping someone up, as an image of kindness; giving a bowl of soup to someone who is hungry as love; or a simple hug as an image of peace. Your images may be entirely different. Wonderful. Go with the images and symbols that resonate with you.

Q: I have often heard the adage to "forgive and forget." How does that perspective fit in with this practice?

A: While that adage might not be completely out of context here, it does have a different focus. "Forgive and forget" is typically centered on moving on from pain and hurt. Loving-kindness reflection is principally concerned with addressing pain and hurt head-on and doing the hard work of going through those deep emotions to find forgiveness and compassion on the other side. Due to that level of engagement, there typically isn't much "forgetting" with loving-kindness reflection, although the sting might be taken out of the remembering.

Q: Is it important to think of others that I have harmed or slighted?

A: Yes, it is an essential piece of this practice because it puts the ways we have been harmed or slighted into perspective. It is easy to become condescending in our "graciousness" to love those who have wronged us until we realize that we have wronged others as well. If we start to think in terms of who has the moral "high ground," then we have already moved far away from the spirit of this practice.

Q: Why can't I start big (i.e., the universe) and work toward small (i.e., an individual)?

A: Experiment. See how that works for you. Going from big to small may have great value for you in loving-kindness reflection. However, I suspect that most of us need to start small—start where we are—so that we don't start at a "big picture," that is, a fictionalized ideal of what we want the world to be rather than the world as it is.

Q: Is there a difference among loving-kindness, tolerance, and acceptance of a wrong?

A: While definitions may shift a bit from person to person, the important difference here is that loving-kindness reflection does not necessitate a specific action as the result of your meditation. Depending on the situation, tolerance might be an acceptable response. At other times, acceptance may be the way to go. Still, at others, loving-kindness could lead to active engagement or resistance.

## POTENTIAL JOURNALING PROMPTS OR DISCUSSION QUESTIONS

1. What positive experiences did you have while practicing this practice?
2. What negative experiences did you have while practicing this practice?
3. How did you adapt this structure to your situation?
4. According to Kabat-Zinn, "[H]ealing is a transformation of view rather than a cure. It involves recognizing your intrinsic wholeness and, simultaneously, your interconnectedness with everything else. Above all, it involves learning to feel at home and at peace within yourself"[4] How does this quote mesh with your experience with loving-kindness reflection? What do *wholeness* and *interconnectedness* mean to you on a personal level?

---

4. Kabat-Zinn, *Full Catastrophic Living*, 217.

# 11

---

# Letting Go

## BRIEF BACKGROUND

It is so easy to hold on to hurt feelings, grudges, disappointments, anger, resentment . . . the list goes on and on. These feelings may block us from listening, especially for subtle moments of contemplation. How can we let go of these feelings that may be so strong that they are physically hurting us? One way is to use the loving-kindness reflection from the previous chapter, but, if you are a bit more visually oriented or hands-on, you might want to try a letting go meditation. These meditations are simple actions to externalize abstract feelings. Without something concrete and tangible, it is often difficult for us to deal with all of the unresolved issues, which block our own spiritual nature.

## HOW TO PRACTICE

### Variant #1: Bubbles

1. Sit down in a comfortable position with your back straight and hands resting on your knees. Close your eyes. Breathe slowly and mindfully for a few breaths.
2. Now imagine your trouble as an object that represents your feeling. If you are having a hard time thinking of an object, try imagining the word itself on a child's set of building blocks.
3. Imagine that object or word inside of a large bubble.
4. Let that bubble float up and away out of sight and out of mind.
5. As it rises, wave it along and wish it well on its journey into nothingness.
6. Take a few more deep breaths and then open your eyes.
7. You may want to practice this visualization multiple times. Don't be hard on yourself. If you don't feel any different after the practice, then just let yourself feel that way.

## Variant #2: Palms Down, Palms Up

1. Sit down in a comfortable position with your back straight and hands resting on your knees. Close your eyes. Breathe slowly and mindfully for a few breaths.
2. Stretch your hands out in front of you with palms down.
3. Pray silently or aloud, naming your feeling to God.
4. Pray silently or aloud, "God, this feeling is hurting me. I need your help. Please be with me through this feeling."
5. Turn your hands palms up as a gesture of receiving help to work through this feeling.
6. Take a few more deep breaths and then open your eyes.
7. Take another moment or two to ponder how it helps to not feel all alone in carrying this feeling.
8. Again, don't be hard on yourself. If you don't feel any different after the practice, then just let yourself feel that way.

## COMMON QUESTIONS

**Q:** What if I don't like bubbles?

**A:** The imagery of the bubble is not absolutely necessary to the activity. However, the imagined action itself might need to change too. For instance, you could imagine your trouble as a heavy stone, which you want to sink in the deepest ocean. You would then want to focus on the sinking of the great weight beneath the waves while you experience a comparative lightness of being. Experiment with different visualizations to see what works for you. Let your imagination run wild.

**Q:** What if I don't like the palms up and palms down activity?

**A:** The same advice as the last answer works here too. Experiment. See whether physical actions or imagined scenarios help you more to focus and stay attentive. Mix and match as desired.

**Q:** How do these practices change the situation that I'm trying to "let go"?

**A:** These practices do not directly change the situation. They are not magic; however, they do have a significant indirect effect on the situation. These practices help to change you and me. We then enter back into our tough life situations and add a new element—the peace that we bring with us. Sometimes, that renewed sense of peace and purpose makes all the difference. These practices do not directly affect the situation. These practices directly affect you and me.

**Q:** What if I have forgiven someone, but my hurt feelings linger?

**A:** First, lingering hurt feelings do not mean that you have failed to forgive. It means that our feelings do not always follow the lead of our will. Forgiveness is an act of our will. It is a choice we make. Feelings don't always cooperate so easily. I recommend acknowledging how you feel. Don't ignore it, gloss over it, or try to run from it. Accept your feeling as your feeling rather than the reality of the situation. That's the first step to moving toward a match of feelings and choices. Be patient with yourself. Feelings catch up to our choices in their own time. Give yourself time.

**Q:** Is it important to tie these meditations to a specific image or physical activity?

**A:** Feel free to experiment with images and activities, but use something tangible. As human beings, we need actions to make the intangible parts of our nature more concrete. Sometimes, we need to see that we've made a choice. We need to see that we have let something go before we'll let ourselves believe that it has really happened. You may have heard that the "devil is in the details." Well, it is also true that "God is met in the rituals." Create your own ritual and find the place of letting go.

## POTENTIAL JOURNALING PROMPTS OR DISCUSSION QUESTIONS

1. What positive experiences did you have while practicing this practice?
2. What negative experiences did you have while practicing this practice?
3. How did you adapt this structure to your situation?
4. How did it feel to let something go that was bothering you?
5. How did it feel to share the burden of your feeling?
6. How did it feel to wish a troubling feeling well as you worked to let it go?

# Section 3

---

# BEING

Why is it so difficult to "be" right here, right now?

Definitions are important—well, at least, I think so. My wife often accuses me of coming up with my own precise definitions and then expecting others to abide by them. I often respond, "What do you mean by 'precise' and 'expecting'?"

All kidding aside, there is some important definitional work for "being" to be done before proceeding to the practices themselves. "Being" in this book is intended to bring to mind the term *mindfulness*, but, first, an explanation of contemplation. Contemplation is the moment when God communicates with an individual, whether it is through words, images, or any other medium. It might be through a burning bush, a descending dove, or even something as simple as the words of a trusted friend—but God is there. Contemplation is most accurately described as an action that *happens* to a participant rather than an action that is *done* by a participant. If we then turn our eyes to the Far East, the most appropriate term to compare with contemplation is enlightenment. In Christian terms, Gautama (the Buddha) experienced contemplation under the Bodhi tree; in Buddhist terms, he obtained enlightenment.

Where does the term *meditation* fit in? Isn't that what all of this is? That's where the definitions get thorny. According to Matthieu Ricard, the term *meditation* in Tibetan "means 'familiarization,' as in 'familiarizing yourself with a new vision of things, a new way to manage your thoughts, of perceiving people and experiencing the world.'"[1] That is a consummate Eastern definition of the term, but it doesn't quite mean the same thing in

---

1. Matthieu Ricard, quoted in Susan Kaiser Greenland, *Mindful Games: Sharing Mindfulness and Meditation with Children, Teens, and Families* (Boulder, CO: Shambhala, 2016), 52.

the West. In Christian usage, meditation does include a "reframing" aspect, but it is more focused on repetition and concentration.

For Christians, meditation is the practice of repeating and thinking over important truths or qualities of God for assimilation into one's spirituality. In this sense, contemplation is a passive activity, and meditation is its active analog. While modern interpretations of meditation have tended to switch the relative meanings of contemplation and meditation, the Christian mystical tradition historically views meditation as active concentration on a particular idea or belief.

When looking back to the Far East, a new term comes into play: *mindfulness*. Susan Kaiser Greenland in her book *Mindful Games* offers a good definition: "The word *mindfulness* comes from the ancient languages Sanskrit and Pali, in which it is defined as 'remembering'—as in remembering the object of our attention."[2] So we can see that mindfulness is closer to the Christian meaning of meditation in the same way that enlightenment is closer to the Christian meaning of contemplation.

Why does all of this matter? I think that foundational definitions like these are important when we push off into the sometimes murky waters of abstraction that spirituality offers to us. Recognition of the different meanings given to these words is vital for cross-cultural conversation. Mindfulness itself is another way of speaking about the practice of becoming aware of where you are right now, of what you're doing right now, of who you are right now—warts and all, with all judging set aside. While I have already introduced some mindful practices, they have focused on filling our minds with content (meditating) or preparing for contemplation (listening). Whether you are called to mindfulness or being, we are going to move to the pure art of learning to pay attention as we take a look at practicing the presence of God, sitting meditation, stargazing, and nonjudging to help us build up our attention spans . . .

---

2. Ibid., 53.

# 12

## Practicing the Presence of God

### BRIEF BACKGROUND

In a similar pattern to centering prayer, the development of a specific mystic practice known as practicing the presence of God can be traced to two particular individuals. The first, and primary, individual to define this mystic practice was the sixteenth-century monk Brother Lawrence. In his small book, *The Practice of the Presence of God*, he outlined his method of viewing every opportunity and activity of the day as a potential moment of intimacy and prayer with God. Through his own experience washing dishes in his monastery, Brother Lawrence described the basics of this practice.

A second individual, Jean-Pierre de Caussade, advocated a similar activity in which a practitioner understood each and every moment as a sacrament in which the grace of God could be communicated to a participant and that participant could communicate with God. As can be seen in this description, practicing the presence of God is a mystic practice which is difficult to consider as a discrete practice that a practitioner would utilize at some times and not use at other times. Therefore, practicing the presence of God is more accurately seen as a settled attitude rather than a specific practice. While phrased in distinctly Christian terms, this practice has general utility for any of us to view each and every moment as sacred and spiritual. No part of our day—or ourselves—is too ordinary to be spiritual.

### HOW TO PRACTICE

There is not necessarily a "right" or "wrong" way to practice the presence of God, since it is more of an attitude. However, to get started, let's try these methods:

## Going on a Walk

Set aside about ten to fifteen minutes. Picture Jesus. Use all five senses to get as clear a picture as possible. Then imagine going on a walk with him. Choose a familiar place. Walk through each step; imagine the space. Imagine Jesus walking with you. Is there anything distinctive about his walk? Visualize a conversation with him. What does he say? How does he say it? What does he want you to remember?

*Note:* If you find your mind wandering during this exercise, then gently concentrate on your breathing, or you could take a page out of the centering prayer method and designate a specific word, such as *here*, to draw your focus back to this visualization.

## Daily Routine

Set aside about ten to fifteen minutes. Picture Jesus. Then picture some familiar place from your daily routine of life. Imagine yourself going through the actions you normally take in the place you normally perform them. Imagine Jesus alongside you. Is he a conversation partner? Is he an active participant? Try to visualize both possibilities. See note above concerning a wandering mind.

## Feelings

Set aside about ten to fifteen minutes. Picture Jesus. Choose at least two different feelings that you have difficulty picturing in Jesus, but you know these feelings in yourself. For instance, can you imagine Jesus being bored? How about confused? Or appreciated? What are Jesus' expressions of these emotions as he is with you? One of the greatest difficulties in practicing the presence of God is that we may often have difficulty believing that God really can experience all of our ups and downs. It helps to picture the range of experience and emotion of Jesus to get past this "pale" version of seeing God with us. Until we can imagine God feeling furious or apathetic with us, we tend to keep him confined to those moments when we are feeling unconditional love and infinite compassion—and how often in a day do we actually feel that way?

# VARIATIONS

1. Set aside about five minutes. Do one of the following: stand on one foot, touch your toes, or pat your head while rubbing your stomach. See how common activities can be quite difficult without practice; see also how common activities become challenging when done for longer and longer stretches of time. Practicing the presence of God is essentially the process of paying attention to spiritual things right here, right now. Ponder how the mundane tasks of your life can be prayer.

2. You can pray like Brother Lawrence: "Lord of all pots and pans and things, make me a saint by getting meals and washing up the plates." You can adapt this prayer to whatever task you are doing at the time.

3. You could also take a page out of the centering prayer method. Designate a simple prayer word of action rather than for meditation and contemplation. For instance, pray the word *here* every so often during your day—just to remind yourself that God is right here, right now.

*Note:* As you might have guessed, there are endless variations to practicing the presence of God. Wherever you go, you can go with God, or at least with a moment-by-moment commitment to believe that God is with you . . . even when you do not "feel" his presence.

# COMMON QUESTIONS

**Q:** How is practicing the presence of God a practice and an attitude?

**A:** The goal, of course, is that practicing God's presence will become a settled attitude for you, but I have experienced that conscious attention must be given to any change of attitude. Think of the "practice" part of practicing the presence of God like building up a habit. The goal of the step-by-step method above is not to keep practicing the presence of God as a discrete practice; rather, it should become a habit—much like putting on your seatbelt when you get into a car. Day after day, you focus on committing to believe that God is with you, and then, one day, you "wake up," and God has been there all along.

**Q:** Can I combine this spiritual practice with other ones?

**A:** Absolutely. Combine this spiritual practice with other spiritual practices or any practice at all, whether you consider it spiritual or secular.

**Q:** What if it feels like I'm not doing anything?

**A:** This practice is susceptible to that feeling much more than other practices. At times when that feeling arises, you might remember the metaphor of habit I mentioned. For instance, you do not need to have any special "feeling" to brush your teeth. It's something you do (hopefully) no matter how you feel. Practicing the presence of God is a spiritual practice for the days when you feel it and for the days when you don't.

**Q:** What if I feel like Jesus is "looking over my shoulder" in a judgmental way?

**A:** I have had more people ask this question than you might think. My advice is to remember that God is with you in this practice, not standing there against you. The practice of the presence of God is not about judgment; it's about not being alone. However, if this shift in mentality is not helpful to you or you sense yourself becoming anxious about being "watched" by God, then this practice might just not be the one for you. Feel free to try something else. You might also consider consulting with a mental health professional concerning feelings of anxiety, if you find that the primary feeling you experience through this practice is an anxious feeling. Sometimes, spiritual practices reveal far more about our emotional and psychological states than spiritual states. That's okay. That may be how God is speaking to you right now. We are holistic beings. Our psychology and spirituality are tied together. A mental health professional can help to uncover psychological sources of anxiety that might be affecting your spiritual life. You might find a counselor who can speak to both the psychological as well as the spiritual aspects of your anxiety.

**Q:** What if I feel like God has "left" me—that I am all alone?

**A:** This practice is not about the felt presence of God as much as it is disciplining our minds and wills to believe—truly believe—that God is with us despite how we might feel in the moment. If you are practicing the presence of God, you may well have moments of feeling the "absence" of God. That is entirely normal in the process. However, if you find that practicing the presence of God raises intense feelings of loneliness or isolation within yourself, then please consult with a mental health professional. Those feelings need to be dealt with on their own, aside from any application to this spiritual practice.

**Q:** Are some actions more conducive than others for practicing the presence of God?

**A:** Not necessarily. However, there definitely are some actions and activities that allow for this practice and awareness more than others when you are first starting out. For instance, I wouldn't start off practicing the presence of God while operating heavy machinery, driving at high speeds, or any activity that requires intense concentration. As you grow in this practice, the hope is that the settled attitude of practicing the presence of God simply becomes second nature to you—you couldn't "switch off" this practice without conscious effort.

**Q:** Does it matter if I sense the presence of Christ rather than the Father, or perhaps some saint or a loved one who has passed away?

**A:** Some people I know prefer a sense of Christ, others the Father, and some the Holy Spirit. It does not alter the practice to meditate on one member of the Trinity over the others, although how you view the practice might be slightly altered. Concerning saints or dead loved ones, that is a bit of a different matter. While I have known some persons who have had a particular saint or the Virgin Mary as a constant inspiration, they would definitely not categorize that sense as "practicing their presence." As for saints and loved ones, that sense would fall more properly under veneration of the saints, which is more like asking a friend to pray for you (to state it in the most basic terms).

**Q:** With this practice in mind, are some activities or kinds of work more holy than others?

**A:** Actually, this practice is intended to help us see exactly the opposite. We can honor God, pray to God, and be with God no matter what work he has given us to do.

**Q:** Do I need to have a sacramental perspective to use this practice?

**A:** That's a hard question to answer. My bottom line answer is no, but—and it's a big *but*—a sacramental perspective greatly enhances practicing the presence of God. To believe that God communicates grace through physical means allows us to believe more easily, and more completely, that God can show grace to you and me through any "physical means" we come into contact with as we go through the day.

# POTENTIAL JOURNALING PROMPTS OR DISCUSSION QUESTIONS

1. What positive experiences did you have while practicing this practice?
2. What negative experiences did you have while practicing this practice?
3. How did you adapt this structure to your situation?
4. What word or phrase did you use as a prayer of action? Why?
5. Were some tasks more conducive to awareness of God's presence than others? Why might that be so?
6. How did you meet God in this practice?
7. Did you notice any change in your behavior during the week as a result of this practice?
8. What benefits might a practice have even if you don't see tangible results right away?

# 13

## Sitting Meditation

### BRIEF BACKGROUND

As defined previously, the term *mindfulness* can be applied to many meditation practices that are common among different religious and spiritual traditions. The most direct source of mindfulness practices comes through the Buddhist tradition, but parallel versions appear in every major world religion. Additionally, mindfulness has become popular in a nonreligious form, which does not specifically tie it to a particular metaphysical worldview. The practice that I will describe here is generic in this sense, and it originates in the pioneering work of Jon Kabat-Zinn. This sitting meditation even has great potential for simple relaxation and stress reduction, even if you don't have a spiritual goal in mind.

### HOW TO PRACTICE

1. Sit in a well-lit, comfortable place with minimal noise and distraction. Try to choose a place where there is little likelihood that you will be interrupted.

2. Assume a comfortable position. For instance, sit in a straight-back chair with feet firmly on the ground. Your hands should be resting on your knees, and you should try to maintain your posture without slouching or resting your back on the back of the chair. You could also sit on the floor in the popular cross-legged posture. Whatever position you choose, make sure that you can sit comfortably for fifteen to twenty minutes without having to rearrange your body too often. You might set a timer, so you are not perpetually looking at the clock.

3. Begin paying attention to your breathing as it flows in and out of your nose. Try not to breathe through your mouth for this exercise. You do

not need to hold your breath. Just breathe naturally, but consciously focus on breathing.

4. Gently close your eyes. If you find that your mind wanders, that's fine. Just bring your attention back to your breath whenever you become aware that you started thinking about something. If you find that your mind wanders a lot, then you might try counting breaths. You might try counting to five for each in-breath and each out-breath. If you have to remind yourself to focus on your breath every few seconds, you have *not* failed. You're not trying to "empty your mind"; just focus on your breathing.

5. At the end of the sitting, you might say or do something to help punctuate the time. For instance, I like to end by quietly saying the word *here* to remind myself that I am always right here in the present no matter where my thoughts might go.

6. You might feel like you are doing a whole lot of nothing, and, if so, great. That's really the point of this spiritual practice. You are learning simply to be.

7. If you stick with this practice, you'll likely notice an increasing calm in your attitude—a willingness not to have to be doing something constantly. Try it out, and see how you like it.

## VARIATIONS

Following the same general steps as above, you can add some variety to your practice in a few ways. Such as:

### Focus on Feeling

After you have learned how to concentrate on your breathing, expand your attention a little. Instead of simply focusing on your breath, be attentive to your entire body. What are you feeling as each breath goes in and out?

### Focus on Hearing

Another possibility is to focus through what you hear. As you breathe in and out and have your eyes closed, what do you hear? You might also try this variation with some soft, soothing music, preferably without words.

## Focus on Thinking

If you find the earlier variations to be easy, you might try actually sitting with your thoughts as a focus for your breathing. Notice a thought as it arises, let it come close, then consciously let it go—like a passing cloud in the sky. For instance, you might be worried about how to pay rent this month. Let that worry arise. Hold it in your mind for a moment. Don't try to solve it. Feel the tension and worry that it causes you. Try to identify where you might feel that tension in your body. Then let the thought "float" away like a cloud. If you find it difficult to let thoughts go in this manner and you begin to obsess about something, then simply go back to being attentive to your breathing.

## Focus on Being

Here's the hardest variation, in my opinion: Just sit. Don't be attentive to thoughts, feelings, sensory information, or even breathing. Simply be. This state of sitting meditation is called choiceless awareness. Don't start with this one, and don't be discouraged if this variation proves quite difficult. Honestly, when I typically try this variation, it often becomes choiceless unconsciousness, sometimes with snoring, so don't be too hard on yourself.

# COMMON QUESTIONS

**Q:** What if I've never done any type of contemplative or meditative practice before?

**A:** First of all, go easy on yourself. Don't expect too much out of the practice until you get used to the "mechanics" of it. Additionally, be aware that you may have thoughts, feelings, or memories surface that are particularly troubling. As mentioned with centering prayer, this circumstance is very common for individuals who struggle with PTSD. If this circumstance happens to you, please consult with a mental health professional. If you do not know a mental health professional, your local priest, pastor, or spiritual leader can recommend one to you.

**Q:** Is this sitting meditation a type of prayer?

**A:** While sitting meditation is not traditionally viewed as a type of prayer, it is a means of becoming more aware. If prayer is viewed as a conversation, then mindfulness does offer some practice in becoming an attentive listener. Still, assigning such a purpose to this mindful practice is going a bit further than it is intended. Learning to "be" is enough for right now.

**Q:** How do I know if this practice is working?

**A:** Mindfulness is "working" if you notice that you are becoming more calm, patient, and aware of the sensations of your body in the present moment. You will feel more grounded in your life, more comfortable in your own skin, and you may not react as quickly to the frustrations of each day. There are subtle effects over time, not drastic changes in a few days. Also, be aware that mindful practices of this sort may bring to your awareness rather uncomfortable feelings. Bringing pain into your awareness might cause it to feel worse before it gets better. If this is the case for you, consider working with a spiritual director or mental health professional as you begin to use this practice.

**Q:** Are there any additional ways of keeping my attention?

**A:** You may bring in some of the other attentive methods from other practices. You might incorporate a particular word or image, like in centering prayer. You also might focus your eyes on your nose even though your eyes are closed. The stillness of your eyes helps to focus your mind. Don't be afraid to experiment with your own personal ways of maintaining attention.

**Q:** What if I keep thinking about something that I can't get out of my mind?

**A:** Note what you are thinking about and the reactions of your mind and body to this thought. Are you feeling anxious? Where do you feel tension in your body? Can you focus on that tense spot and imagine just letting it relax? Typically in mindfulness you focus on sensations of your body or your own breath in order to get away from obsessive thoughts.

**Q:** What if I spend the whole time "fighting" with my thoughts?

**A:** Don't be too hard on yourself. That happens to everyone sometimes. In fact, one of the most valuable purposes of sitting meditation is showing you how much you really do "fight" your thoughts all the time. Become aware that you are fighting—don't judge whether it is good or bad, simply observe—and then move on.

**Q:** What if I fall asleep?

**A:** Actually, sitting meditation is the most common practice to end in falling asleep, so don't set unrealistic expectations. If you find yourself falling asleep every time, then vary the time of day you practice or your position during the practice. If I am particularly tired, I like to sit on the floor while I meditate. It is slightly uncomfortable for me, and that's just enough to keep me from getting sleepy. Experiment with different positions to find what might be that "slightly uncomfortable" spot for you.

**Q:** What if I have a mystical experience during sitting meditation?

**A:** Great. Write it down. Ponder on it. What insights might you gain, or others gain, through it? However, remember that having a mystical experience is not the purpose of this practice. Moment-by-moment awareness and simple presence—actually paying attention to where we are right now—is the main purpose. Keep an eye to that aim.

**Q:** What if I don't feel like I'm doing anything?

**A:** I guarantee that you'll feel this way part of the time. It feels so alien in our fast-paced culture to take time out to do nothing—and to actually do nothing. See if you can settle into a state of simple attentiveness, or as Jon Kabat-Zinn likes to call it, "falling awake," and, perhaps, make a note of how surprising it is that simple boredom can make you so uncomfortable.

## POTENTIAL JOURNALING PROMPTS OR DISCUSSION QUESTIONS

1. What positive experiences did you have while practicing this practice?
2. What negative experiences did you have while practicing this practice?
3. How did you adapt this structure to your situation?
4. What could be the benefits of learning to just be in your life?
5. Was it difficult to be alone with yourself in this practice? How? Why?
6. Sitting meditation is often coupled with other spiritual practices. What spiritual practices would you like to try combining with it? When could you try out that combination this week?

# 14

## Stargazing

### BRIEF BACKGROUND

Most of the mindfulness practices that I have presented so far have been intent on helping us to focus in the sense of centering and narrowing our attention. It is also helpful to mindfully practice the widening of our attention. If we liken the previous practices to focusing our attention like a laser beam, then stargazing is comparable to the diffusing warmth of a lazy sunbeam on a summer's day.

### HOW TO PRACTICE

As you follow these steps, try to hold in your mind that we are exploring the present moment, right here, right now:

1. Sit or lie down outside where you can comfortably gaze at the night sky. Get comfortable and briefly bring your attention to your breathing. Take five deep breaths.

2. While you may have gone stargazing before to spot particular planets or constellations, this is a bit different. Look toward the horizon, but don't stare. Comfortably look at the horizon point, and then slowly broaden your focus to become aware of more and more of the night sky. Eventually, let yourself see all of it at once.

3. Don't focus on any one object, but note when a change in the sky registers in your mind. It might be a change in the moon, stars, or sky. Notice how even a slight shift of your position can change your perspective on the scope of the sky.

4. When a thought arises, don't ignore it and don't chase it. Just let it be.

5. When a feeling arises, don't ignore it and don't chase it. Just let it be.

6. You may stargaze as long as you like, but try to spend at least fifteen minutes in the practice at first. If you do not have any other time limitations, strive for a period of time that allows you to settle into this practice of broadening attention in which you stay to the point of getting slightly uncomfortable. If you are starting to pay more attention to the little aches and pains of your body than to the sky, then it's time to conclude the practice.

7. At the end of the practice, spend a few more moments concentrating on your breathing to bring your attention back from the broadening of your perspective.

## VARIATIONS

The various steps of stargazing can be adapted to any wide vista that you may see before you in your everyday life. For example, stargazing can easily become forest gazing, cloud gazing, or city skyline gazing. The point is to look up and see the broader perspective. Experiment with the context to find what resonates most deeply for you.

## COMMON QUESTIONS

**Q:** Why is this practice categorized as one of "focus" and "attention"?

**A:** It does seem oddly different from how we are used to thinking of attention. However, our attention, like our own perspectives, benefits from occasional widening as well as narrowing. This practice helps us to learn to pay attention in daily life to not "miss the forest for the trees," as the old adage goes. Most other mindfulness practices approach attention from the other direction, so we don't miss the trees for the forest, so to speak.

**Q:** What if I find myself falling asleep or "spacing out" during the practice?

**A:** Falling asleep or spacing out are common occurrences in the first few sessions of using this practice. However, this practice is actually very different from spacing out. You are deliberately holding your attention on its "panoramic" setting. In spacing out, you simply stop paying attention. If you find that you have spaced out, simply take a few deep breaths and try to get back on track with your "wide angle lens" perspective. If you find yourself perpetually falling asleep, then you might try a different practice. In the interest of full disclosure, I don't use this practice very often. I am an early morning person, so by the time the stars roll out if I were to lay down without moving for any length of time, then I would rapidly fall asleep.

**Q:** What if I find this practice to be especially difficult for me?

**A:** While some practitioners have initial troubles with spacing out or falling asleep as noted above, some people have great difficulty in the process of widening out their attention. That result is not unexpected. Honestly, how often do we practice widening our attention in everyday life? We might be told "Pay attention" several times in a day, but each time the emphasis is on narrowing attention to a specific task, not widening our focus to take in the vast expanse of the big picture. Widening attention can prove to be a difficult skill to learn, but it brings rewards of its own that we simply cannot get without taking the time to look up and look out.

**Q:** What if thoughts or feelings are particularly distracting me from broadening my attention?

**A:** Thoughts and feelings often fade away on their own if we just don't focus on them. However, occasionally, something might be troubling you so intently that it seems impossible to think or feel anything else. At those times, you might try visualizing your thoughts and feelings in the midst of a fast-moving river. Let the current sweep those distractions away while you draw your attention back to the starry sky.

**Q:** What about "crowd gazing" or "people watching"?

**A:** I have not listed "crowd gazing" as one of my recommended variations because the movement of people tends to distract from the relaxation that is at the foundation of this practice. Stars, clouds, forests, and even city lights tend to move less chaotically than we human beings. Perhaps that insight is worth pondering on its own.

**Q:** Is there anything particularly important about the role of stars in the practice?

**A:** You can use this mindfulness meditation with other foci, but I find that starting with stars is particularly meaningful. When you contemplate the stars, you are seeing the light that has been traveling here for untold millennia. When you mindfully gaze at the stars, you are broadening your attention not only in terms of space but also in terms of time. It is quite beautiful when you stop to think about it.

**Q:** What if I have difficulty in integrating the bigness of what I see with the smallness of my individual viewpoint?

**A:** Gazing at the stars, whether mindfully or even more generally, helps us all gain an essential element of perspective concerning our place in the grand scheme of the universe: the element of humility. Don't fight that perspective; embrace it.

## POTENTIAL JOURNALING PROMPTS OR DISCUSSION QUESTIONS

1. What positive experiences did you have while practicing this practice?
2. What negative experiences did you have while practicing this practice?
3. Were you surprised by anything you saw?
4. Did the sky seem more to stay the same or to change?
5. What would change in your life if you practiced stargazing as a habit?
6. How did you adapt the practice to your situation?

# 15

## Nonjudging

### BRIEF BACKGROUND

One of the foundational pillars of mindfulness practice is the stance of non-judgmental awareness. In this stance, we realize all of the little judgment calls we make every day. Often these calls are a matter of distinguishing our own preferences rather than anything inherently negative; however, it is easy to immerse ourselves in judging viewpoints and then mindlessly bring them to our interactions with other people individually and in community. We can build our awareness of our own judgments and how that mindset negatively impacts those around us with the practice of nonjudging. By using the proceeding steps to practice consciously withholding judgment, you can build the necessary space to pause and choose whether you will judge or not rather than reacting without thinking.

### HOW TO PRACTICE

What do we do when other people get on our nerves? Here's a possibility:

1. Think of someone with whom you have had a disagreement recently. It is best to start small at first. Don't go straight to your "arch enemy."
2. Try to remember the moment of disagreement. How did you feel? Be specific.
3. Now let's step outside ourselves for a moment. How do you imagine the other person felt?
4. Before going any further, think of three things you have in common. They can be large or small. They can have bearing on your disagreement or be totally irrelevant to your argument. Think of them now. Perhaps even write them down. One. Two. Three.
5. Take five deep breaths to focus on each of those things in common.

6. Do not try to progress from this point to rationalize your actions or demonize the other person's actions. No excuses. No justifications. The point here is not even to forgive or move past those actions. Simply hold before your mind the matters you have in common.

7. Throughout the rest of the day, try to remind yourself from time to time of those things you hold in common. Let those three things be your meditation, your mantra for today.

## VARIATIONS

Sometimes you may find yourself in the enviable position of not being able to think of a particular disagreement or hurt feeling you have toward another person. During those times, try this variation:

1. Visualize a ball, or, better yet, go get a ball to use in this practice.

2. Imagine the good thoughts and well wishes you have for others in a general sense. These wishes can be as general or specific as you like. If you desire all people to have full bellies, warm beds, and world peace, then now is the time to make that wish.

3. With each wish, imagine the ball as a bit heavier as you place your thought, your energy, within it.

4. Visualize other people holding the ball with you: friends, family, coworkers, classmates, acquaintances, strangers, even enemies if you like.

5. Imagine the energy from all of you flowing into the ball, filling it with well wishes and getting correspondingly heavier.

6. Take five deep breaths. Then toss the ball up, figuratively or literally. Imagine the wishes and thoughts spreading up into the sky, diffusing in the air, circling the globe, and raining down on all people in the world.

7. Throughout the rest of the day, try to remind yourself from time to time of the image of the ball, that big, friendly ball bringing good thoughts to the planet. Notice how holding that thought before your mind—just the thought—might affect your behavior in the present moment.

*Note:* While these variations direct our minds to others, you can also utilize these methods to practice nonjudging toward yourself. We can often be our own worst critics; step back from judging yourself today.

## COMMON QUESTIONS

**Q:** What if I don't feel like I'm doing anything?

**A:** While this question applies to many mindfulness practices, it is especially pertinent here because if you are asking this question, then it is time for a change in perspective. The major point in this practice is that kindness should be prioritized over results. Having wrongs righted or feeling acknowledged is incomplete without seeing our connections with everyone else.

**Q:** Isn't this a variation on the loving-kindness reflection (chapter 10)?

**A:** Yes, it is. You can use these practices alternately or in combination.

**Q:** What if I can't think of three things I have in common with the other person?

**A:** It can be very difficult to think of things you have in common with a person with whom you are angry. Don't let that become an excuse. Also, don't try to circumvent the point of the practice by being "snarky." Of course, we all breathe, eat, sleep, etc. Go deeper than the obvious. However, if you honestly cannot think of three points you have in common, go talk to that person. Do not speak about the hurt if you can avoid it; ask them about what you have in common. You might be surprised at where the conversation might head from there.

**Q:** What if my feelings toward that person or situation aren't changing?

**A:** That's perfectly normal. This practice is not about changing your feelings toward the person, although change does happen in many cases. The aim of the practice is to widen your perspective, not to change how you feel.

**Q:** Why is this a "spiritual" practice?

**A:** Spiritual practices often focus on our interaction with God or ultimate reality of some sort. While most of the practices in this book follow that focus, I offer a few practices that are more interpersonal in nature. Our relationship with God is not disconnected from our other relationships as much as we might think. In fact, we may even experience God only through the context of our relationships with other human beings. Everything is interconnected.

**Q:** What if I start with the variation instead of the initial steps you suggested?

**A:** It's easier to start with the warm, soft fuzziness of the "human race." Do the hard work of starting with the individual human being whom you know. If you want to start the other way around, go ahead and experiment. Either way, we always need to deal with the individuals in our lives as well as the larger community. Both are necessary.

**Q:** I have often heard the adage to "forgive and forget." How does that perspective fit in with this practice?

**A:** While that adage might not be completely out of context here, it does have a different focus. "Forgive and forget" is typically centered on moving on from the pain and slight. I don't mention anything about forgiveness in this practice. Nonjudging is not about forgiveness. In fact, the decision to forgive someone is a judgment call itself. Nonjudging comes first. It might make forgiveness easier, but that's not its purpose. This practice is about your perspective, not your action toward another person. Too often, we rush into forgiveness or trying to forget without addressing our own perspective over the whole issue. Such rushing assures that we will have to face the same problems over and over again. Break the cycle by seeing differently.

## POTENTIAL JOURNALING PROMPTS OR DISCUSSION QUESTIONS

1. What is your role in the disagreement? (Be honest.)
2. What are your good thoughts and well wishes?
3. How would you feel if someone did these practices with something you've done to them?
4. How does this practice teach us about interdependence?
5. How does this practice teach us about the nature of change?
6. What are some ways that we are all connected with each other?

# Section 4

## SENSING

An overwhelming majority of the practices shared in previous chapters are about sitting still and paying attention. While a few active practices have slipped in here and there, you may be tempted to conclude at this point that spirituality and mystic practice bears a striking resemblance to being in "time-out" long enough to "consider the consequences of your actions." Well, take heart. You are not in trouble, nor are you alone in feeling that mystic practices are a tad heavy on the sedentary side of life.

Spiritual practices from all traditions tend to stress helping us to be still and listen to the quiet whispers of divinity or ultimate reality that are ever present. The reason for this emphasis is that we often do not seem to need the same kind of motivation (and instruction) in realizing the need to move. In many ways, it seems that motion is our default setting in the fast-paced world of today. So if we were to start with the most active spiritual practices, then we may never find the time to get around to the quieter, less visible, and more easily forgotten practices in the sections of meditating, listening, and being.

With the appropriate foundation laid, however, we can now proceed for the remainder of this book to consider spiritual practices that entail some element of action. In this section, we will begin where we left off from the last section: attention. If the previously profiled practices have indeed helped us to build up our attention, then let's use that attention as we move into our bodies. The way forward for us is through our five senses: sight, hearing, smell, taste, and touch. These practices are the most tactile practices arising out of various religious traditions. So let's dig into the Rosary, praying with icons, body scan, mindful eating, drumbeat, fasting, labyrinths, and pilgrimage. If you were expecting something a bit more vigorous than the practices on this list, then just flip to section 5. We'll learn to embody our senses in this section, and we'll put everything together into an entire body "flow" in the next section.

# 16

---

# The Rosary

## BRIEF BACKGROUND

In much the same vein as the Jesus Prayer, the mystic practice of the Rosary has historically centered on the use of specific prayers by an individual to aid meditation and contemplation. While the Jesus Prayer may occasionally be accompanied with the use of a prayer rope, the use of the Rosary has been linked particularly closely to the use of rosary beads. In fact, it is common to refer to the Rosary and mean the beads, not the prayers associated with them. These beads allow the practitioner to keep count of the number of prayers according to the specified number for that particular Rosary prayer. There are many different types of prayer beads throughout history, but the two most common varieties in Christian spirituality are the Roman Catholic Rosary and the Anglican Rosary. Notably, the Roman Catholic Rosary uses beads that are separated into ten beads or "decades," which are in turn separated by larger beads which remind the participant to meditate on different mysteries of the Christian faith. Anglican Rosaries use beads which have four sections of seven beads, called "weeks," instead of five sections of ten and slightly different prayers, but the purpose of Anglican Rosaries and Roman Catholic Rosaries is essentially the same. As with the Jesus Prayer, the historical purpose of the Rosary is to drive out distractions, focus on God, or meditate on the mysteries of the Christian faith.

## HOW TO PRACTICE (This example uses the Anglican Rosary.)

Various prayers may be used with the Rosary or in the same manner as the Rosary. The most traditional prayers are:

- *The Ave Maria* ("Hail Mary"): Hail Mary, full of grace; the Lord is with you: blessed are you among women, and blessed is the fruit of your womb, Jesus. Holy Mary, mother of God, pray for us sinners, now and at the hour of our death. *Amen.*

- *The "Our Father" or "Lord's Prayer":* Our Father, who art in heaven, hallowed be thy name. Thy kingdom come. Thy will be done on earth as it is in heaven. Give us this day our daily bread. Forgive us our trespasses as we forgive those who trespass against us, and lead us not into temptation, but deliver us from evil. For thine is the kingdom, and the power, and the glory. Forever and ever. *Amen.* (Matt. 6:9–13).

- *The "Prayer of St. Francis":* Lord, make me an instrument of your peace. Where there is hatred, let me sow love; where there is injury, pardon; where there is doubt, faith; where there is despair, hope; where there is darkness, light; and where there is sadness, joy. O Divine Master, grant that I may not so much seek to be consoled as to console; to be understood as to understand; to be loved as to love. For it is in giving that we receive; it is in pardoning that we are pardoned; and it is in dying that we are born to eternal life. *Amen.*

*Note*: Feel free, however, to use any other prayers that are meaningful to you. Many wonderful prayers are available in the Roman Catholic missal, the Episcopal Book of Common Prayer, or any anthology of prayers.

1. Begin by meditating on the pendant, usually a cross, for a few minutes. The pendant should be resting in your hand.

2. Then address God as follows, "Glory be to the Father, Son, and Holy Spirit. Amen." while making the sign of the cross. This short prayer is known as the "Glory be."

3. Move from the pendant to the first large bead, called the Invitatory bead, directly after the pendant. At this point, say the "Our Father." You are inviting God to be with you in your prayers.

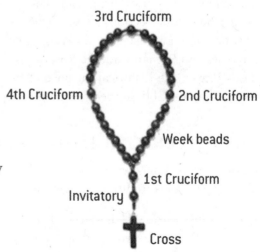

3rd Cruciform

4th Cruciform

2nd Cruciform

Week beads

1st Cruciform

Invitatory

Cross

4. After saying the "Our Father," move to the next large bead, called the first cruciform bead. At this point say another "Glory be."

5. Then, move to the first group of smaller beads, called a week. For each bead, pray the Jesus Prayer, Ave Maria, or other desired prayer. Don't rush through the prayer. Try saying one word per breath.

6. When you make it through all seven smaller beads in the group and you make it to the second cruciform bead, say another "Glory be."

7. Repeat this process of saying the "Glory be" on the cruciform beads and the Jesus Prayer, Ave Maria, etc. on each week bead until you return again to the first cruciform bead. End the prayer time by saying the "Our Father" once again.

## VARIATIONS

While the Roman Catholic Rosary is typically prayed in a very specific way without alteration, there are many different prayers which one can use in order to pray the Anglican Rosary. It is for this reason that I have built my "How to Practice" section around the Anglican Rosary rather than the older and more widely used Roman Catholic Rosary. The resources on page 218 can provide further options. You may also find value in creating prayers of your own or adapting prayers from the Book of Common Prayer to use with the Rosary. Remember the Rosary and its beads are tools to aid you in the memorization and counting of prayers. The use of these tools is really only limited by your imagination.

## COMMON QUESTIONS

**Q:** What if I've never practiced this type of prayer before?

**A:** Don't expect too much out of the practice until you get used to the "mechanics" of it. Realize that this type of prayer practice has results that are seen more in your attitude throughout the day rather than during the practice itself.

**Q:** What if I don't feel anything?

**A:** This is a common question that applies to almost any practice. Rest assured that these practices are not about certain feelings. Feelings come and go. At times, you may have very intense feelings while praying the Rosary. At other times, you might not feel anything special at all. Feelings will vary from time to time and from person to person. Find your own rhythm.

**Q:** Do I need prayer beads to use the Rosary prayers?

**A:** No, you can use the prayers and any associated meditations without the beads. The beads only help add a kinesthetic facet to your actions. That piece is often very helpful for those of us who need to keep our hands busy in order to keep our minds focused.

**Q:** What if I lose the count?

**A:** That's completely fine. The specific number of prayers is not as important as the intention and the repetitive action. You can simply begin again or pick up wherever you last were sure of the count, typically at a cruciform bead.

**Q:** How often should I go through all the prayers of the Rosary?

**A:** There is not a set amount, and you are not necessarily more "holy" if you go through the prayers more often. Here is another chance to find your own rhythm. Experiment. See what works for you. As with the Jesus Prayer, I offer a word of caution: if you suffer from obsessive compulsive disorder (OCD), then this might not be the practice for you. If you begin to feel a compulsion to get a certain number of prayers into your day for the specific reason of attaining a certain number, then this practice may have become counterproductive for you. Simply set it aside, and try something else for a while.

**Q:** How quickly should I go through the whole round of prayers?

**A:** The amount of time is really up to you. I have sped through them in about ten minutes, and I have taken well over an hour to move slowly and meditatively through each repetition. Some people spend quite a bit of time meditating on the prayer or image they choose to associate with each cruciform bead. Whether you take minutes or hours, it is up to you to judge what feels right to you. However, I do encourage you to try a long prayer period with the Rosary, at least once, just to see how it strikes you.

**Q:** Do you have to be Catholic to use the Roman Catholic Rosary, or do you have to be an Episcopalian to use the Anglican Rosary?

**A:** No, however, the content of some of the prayers may be more suited to your particular theological perspective if you use prayers from your own tradition. Prayer beads are actually used as a tool in many different religions, including Hinduism, Buddhism, and Islam. As you might guess, the number of prayers and number of beads vary a little, but the content of the prayers is the real subject of change.

**Q:** Is it wrong to wear prayer beads as jewelry?

**A:** No, in fact, wearing either necklace-sized Rosary beads or bracelet-sized Rosary beads is an excellent reminder of your prayers when you are not able to sit down and have a time set aside to pray.

**Q:** Are there specific subjects I should meditate on when I get to the cruciform beads?

**A:** You can meditate on whatever you like, but there are traditional meditations known as "mysteries" that are associated with the different cruciform beads and which change according to the day of the week in Catholic tradition. These mysteries consist of significant events from the lives of Jesus and Mary. If you are interested in learning more about the mysteries, please consult John Phalen's *Living the Rosary: Finding Your Life in the Mysteries*, listed in the "Resources for Further Study" on page 218.

## POTENTIAL JOURNALING PROMPTS OR DISCUSSION QUESTIONS

1. What positive experiences did you have while practicing this practice?
2. What negative experiences did you have while practicing this practice?
3. How did you adapt this structure to your situation?
4. How did you meet God in this practice?
5. How did the repetitive nature of this practice impact you?
6. How did the Ave Maria (or whichever prayer you chose) encourage you to think differently this week?
7. How did the physical act of using the rosary beads help you to pray this week?

# 17

## Praying with Icons

### BRIEF BACKGROUND

An icon is a two-dimensional artistic representation of a religious scene or personage for the express purpose of aiding a practitioner in prayer. The icon is used as a focal point for prayers on the person or event depicted in the icon. Both "writing" (i.e., painting) an icon and "reading" (i.e., praying with) an icon can be considered a mystical practice. Writing an icon involves particular prayers one uses while painting in a very structured manner in order to produce the desired artistic result. Use of an icon in prayer is theologically intended to draw you into the reality of the person or event depicted through the icon itself. Resultantly, both of these activities find a place for implementation in the mystical tradition as a means in which you might meet God.

This exercise is simply based on praying with an icon. If you are interested in "writing" an icon, please see bibliographic information below for Peter Pearson's *A Brush with God: An Icon Workbook*. This step-by-step guide is the best one that I have found to walk you through every step of the way in creating an icon. Pearson also conducts icon workshops on a regular basis. Consult his website (*http://pfpbilltown.wixsite.com/new-website*) to schedule or attend a workshop.

### HOW TO PRACTICE

1. Spend some time gazing at the icon of Christ shown here.
2. What features stand out to you? For example, notice the position of Jesus' hands. What is Jesus holding? Where is Jesus looking?
3. Now spend some time applying those things to your life. What do these features say to you in your experience right now?

4. Move deeper into the picture. Ask more metaphorical and probing questions. For example, why isn't Jesus smiling? Why isn't there a nail print in Jesus' hand? What does the background tell you?

5. Ask more personal questions. For example, what is Christ teaching you? What is Christ thinking about? How do you meet Christ through these features? What is he saying to you?

## VARIATIONS

There is great potential for variation within the basic steps of this method. Choose different icons from the wide variety available in Christianity that have been created since the earliest centuries. Additionally, do not feel bound to the steps I outlined above. My purpose in these steps is simply to give you a foundation for how to draw your attention to the icon and the spiritual reality that it represents. Experiment. Adapt. Explore.

## COMMON QUESTIONS

Q: Why are icons painted in such a stylized manner?

A: There are actually very precise theological reasons for almost every part of an icon— down to line, color, arrangement, and even geometry. Icons are often described as "windows into heaven" through which we can peer into a deeper reality. If that perspective intrigues you, then I encourage you to check out some of the books in the "Resources for Further Study" section on page 219. However, at this point, let me reassure you that it is not necessary to know all of the intricate details of the style of an icon in order to use one effectively in prayer. Try praying with icons. If this practice resonates with you, then find out more about it. Don't be afraid to begin without knowing everything about this practice.

**Q:** Is it necessary to have a sacramental theology in order to use icons in prayer?

**A:** While it is not absolutely necessary, a sacramental view of nature—that God speaks through the physical reality all around us—is intricately bound up with the history and tradition of icons. Perhaps you could experiment with this viewpoint as you pray. What if God's grace could come to you through something as simple as a painting? Of course, if this possibility is distasteful to you, then you can simply move on to another contemplative practice.

**Q:** Can I use artistic representations of Christ and the events of the Christian religion that are not icons in the same way?

**A:** I do not recommend using artwork that is not iconographic as an icon. Icons were developed specifically for praying in this way. The details are meant to speak through meditative gazing and prayer. If you wish to use another type of artwork, I recommend that you use it according to the variations noted under the practice of centering prayer. That practice would likely fit your purpose better.

**Q:** Is there a similar spiritual purpose or result for "writing" and "reading" an icon?

**A:** While these two spiritual activities are closely related, they can strike a participant quite differently. My advice is to try both, and see what happens. Also, if you feel that you have little artistic talent, then do not feel that "writing" an icon is not for you. Icon creation is highly structured, and it is much more craft than art, as far as skill levels are concerned. It's a bit like an ancient version of "paint-by-number." Try creating an icon, if you have the opportunity. You might be surprised at how deeply spiritual of a process it is for you.

**Q:** Doesn't the Bible warn against "graven images" (Exod. 20:4–6)? How is an icon different from a graven image?

**A:** One of the most important controversies of the church, the iconoclast controversy, happened over that question in the eighth century. Briefly stated, the church decided that icons were different in nature from graven images, and they did not receive worship; rather, the praying participant was worshiping the reality that was only depicted in the icon. The icon might participate in that reality, but it was not that reality itself. For a longer explanation, please consult Ambrosios

Giakalis' book, *Images of the Divine: The Theology of Icons at the Seventh Ecumenical Council.*

**Q:** Is there a correct posture to pray with icons or a particular point to fix my gaze?

**A:** No, there is not one right way to position oneself or one's eyes in this practice. Many people do kneel as they pray with icons. Others stand. Some sit. Find what works for you. Concerning one's gaze, some find a fixed point in the icon on which to meditate. Others let their eyes rove. I've used both methods, and I've gazed at different points of the same icon during different prayer times. It's up to your own preferences how you want to adapt the posture of your body and your eyes.

**Q:** Should I verbalize any part of my prayers as I pray with an icon?

**A:** Feel free to do so, if you like; however, there are no specific admonitions to pray certain prayers aloud in connection with gazing at an icon. On the other hand, there are no admonitions to be silent either. As with most of the contemplative practices outlined in this section, a practitioner is more often silent than not when using these practices, but it is seldom a hard-and-fast rule. Interpret this practice as you see fit.

## POTENTIAL JOURNALING PROMPTS OR DISCUSSION QUESTIONS

1. What positive experiences did you have while practicing this practice?
2. What negative experiences did you have while practicing this practice?
3. How did you adapt this structure to your situation?
4. How did you meet God in this practice?
5. What symbols spoke to you in the icon? What did these symbols mean to you?
6. How did praying with the use of an icon help you to be more attentive to the symbols in everyday life during the week?

# 18

## Body Scan

### BRIEF BACKGROUND

In a manner similar to *lectio divina*, there are many variations of mindfulness practices. In addition to the sitting meditation that I have outlined in chapter 13, the body scan is a wonderful foundational practice. It is my personal favorite way to practice mindfulness as a discrete activity. Jon Kabat-Zinn masterfully describes how to begin this practice in his magnum opus, *Full Catastrophe Living*, so I will adapt his steps at length here. Anyone interested in going further with mindfulness should definitely consult his many, many works on the subject.

### HOW TO PRACTICE

1. Lie down on your back in a comfortable place, such as on a foam mat on the floor or on your bed. Keep in mind from the very beginning that in this lying-down practice, the intention is to "fall awake" rather than to fall asleep. Make sure that you will be warm enough. You might want to cover yourself with a blanket if the room is cold.

2. Allow your eyes to gently close. If, however, you find any drowsiness creeping in, feel free to open your eyes and continue with them open.

3. Gently let your attention settle on your abdomen, feel the rise and fall of your belly with each inhalation and each exhalation; in other words, "riding the waves" of your own breathing with full awareness for the full duration of each inbreath and the full duration of each outbreath.

4. Take a few moments to feel your body as a whole, from head to toe; the "envelope" of your skin; the sensations associated with touch in the places you are in contact with the floor or the bed.

5. Bring your attention to the toes of your left foot. As you direct your attention to them, see if you can direct or channel your breathing to them as well, so that it feels as if you are breathing in to your toes and out from your toes. It may take a while for you to get the hang of this so that it doesn't feel forced or contrived. It may help to imagine your breath traveling down the body from your nose into the lungs and continuing through the torso and down the left leg all the way to the toes, and then back again and out through your nose. Actually, the breath does take this and every other route in the body, through the bloodstream.

6. Allow yourself to feel any and all sensations from your toes, perhaps distinguishing between them and observing the changing sensations in this region. In paying attention to that area, be careful not to judge what you are experiencing. Simply notice the sensations, and let them be.

7. When you are ready to leave the toes and move on, take a deeper, more intentional breath in all the way down to the toes and, on the outbreath, allow them to "dissolve" in your mind's eye. Stay with your breathing for a few breaths at least, and then move on in turn to the sole of the foot, the heel, the top of the foot, and then the ankle, continuing to breathe in to and out from each region as you observe the sensations that you are experiencing, and then letting go of that region and moving on.

8. As with the sitting meditation practice, bring your mind back to the breath and to the region you are focusing on each time you notice that your attention has wandered off, after first taking note of what carried you away in the first place or what is on your mind when you realize it has wandered away from the focus on the body.

9. In this way, continue moving slowly up your left leg and through the rest of your body as you maintain the focus on the breath and on the sensations within the individual regions as you come to them, breathe with them, and let go of them.

10. When you finally make it to the top of your head, breathe into your entire body for a rhythm of five deep inhalations and exhalations. Then allow your body to emerge from this settled state of relaxation and awareness.

11. Try to practice the body scan at least once a day while you are testing this practice to see if it fits you. Kabat-Zinn's patients in his Mindfulness-Based Stress Reduction Clinic do the body scan forty-five minutes a day, six days a week, for at least the first two weeks of their training.

12. The most important point is to get down on the floor and practice. How much or for how long is not as important as making the time for it at all, every day if possible.[1]

## COMMON QUESTIONS

**Q:** What if I fall asleep?

**A:** It is very common to end in falling asleep, so don't set unrealistic expectations. If you find yourself falling asleep every time, then vary the time of day you practice or your position during the practice. Personally, while many resources advocate lying down while doing a body scan, I simply cannot do it. I prefer to do a body scan in a seated position, either sitting on my heels or in a cross-legged position. Both of these positions are "slightly" uncomfortable for me after twenty to thirty minutes. Experiment with what positions work that way for you. You might even try combining the body scan with one or more of the yoga poses that I suggest in chapter 25.

**Q:** What if I feel like I'm not doing anything?

**A:** You'll feel this way part of the time. It feels so alien in our fast-paced culture to take time out to do nothing—and to actually do nothing. Try to settle into a state of simple attentiveness, or as Jon Kabat-Zinn likes to call it, "falling awake," and, perhaps, make a note of how surprising it is that simple boredom can make you so uncomfortable.

**Q:** What if I don't have any sensations from a particular body part or region?

**A:** Don't be alarmed. That is quite normal. Just allow yourself to feel "not feeling anything." Gaining the awareness of what you do not feel in the sensations of your own body is just as important as increasing awareness of more noticeable sensations. The end result is more cumulative. Little by little, you will be paying attention to the constant stream of

---

1. Adapted from Jon Kabat-Zinn's *Full Catastrophe Living*, 95–97.

information that your body is feeding to you. You are learning to be—
just be—in the present. That can take quite a bit of hard work.

**Q:** What if I don't have time to go through every little body part (e.g., toes, sole of foot, heel of foot, top of foot, etc.)?

**A:** It is perfectly fine to group body parts together if pressed for time. For instance, I often focus my awareness on my entire foot rather than its component parts. Also, you may desire focusing on only one body area rather than an entire body scan. This piecemeal version of a body scan is quite common in pain management therapies.

**Q:** Do I have to lie down?

**A:** No. As I mentioned above, lying down is not my preferred way to practice a body scan. Find what works for you. Remember to just begin and feel free to make adjustments along the way. Change the practice to suit you; don't change yourself to suit the practice.

**Q:** Do I need absolute quiet for this practice?

**A:** I recommend starting with complete quiet or soft music because you will need more concentration than you expect to focus on being aware of your sensations from one part of your body at a time. However, once you have built a habit, you may find it easier to practice a body scan in noisier or more crowded environments. Still, it works best in quiet and solitude.

**Q:** Can I do a body scan while moving?

**A:** Most of the time, I recommend adapting a practice however you prefer, but this is one case where I do not follow that pattern. I have attempted to do a body scan while moving, and it becomes more of a "check-in" to make sure everything is operating smoothly. That check-in can be useful in multiple circumstances (e.g., jogging), but it is difficult to maintain a meditative attitude simultaneously. Still, you might try it and have more success than me, but that has been my experience.

**Q:** What if I feel "blocked" at a certain point in my body? (Blocking could be a sense of energy or more physical in nature—stiffness, burning, tingling, itching, aching, etc.)

**A:** Feelings of blockage, or even pain, are not at all uncommon. If you cannot identify an obvious cause for these feelings and sensations, then you might consult with a mental health professional that has experience in mindfulness-based therapy. Your body might be telling you something that you would rather ignore or forget.

**Q:** What if I experience feelings of anxiety during the body scan?

**A:** We tend to "store" our anxiety and tension in our bodies, so such a response is quite possible. If, however, you are experiencing persistent periods of anxiety or a strong, overwhelming "attack" of anxiety, then please consult with a mental health professional. As mentioned in the last answer, it helps if that person also has experience with mindfulness-based therapy.

**Q:** What if I have moments of psychological breakthrough or mystical experience while doing a body scan?

**A:** Great. Write it down. Ponder on it. What insights might you gain, or others gain, through it? However, remember that experience is not the purpose of mindfulness practice. Moment-by-moment awareness and simple presence—actually paying attention to where we are right now—is the main purpose. Keep an eye to that aim.

## POTENTIAL JOURNALING PROMPTS OR DISCUSSION QUESTIONS

1. What positive experiences did you have while practicing this practice?
2. What negative experiences did you have while practicing this practice?
3. How did you adapt this structure to your situation?
4. What could be the benefits of learning to just be in your body?
5. Was it difficult to focus on how each part of your body felt in this practice? How? Why?

# 19

## Mindful Eating

### BRIEF BACKGROUND

Another mindfulness practice that is easy to integrate into your everyday life is mindful eating. In this practice, you are consciously bringing your awareness—your moment-to-moment attention—to a wonderful sensory process that each of us do every day. Yet eating is an activity that so many of us do in an excessively mindless way. In fact, a major cause of overeating is that we are not paying attention to the signals which our body is giving us to indicate that we are full. Give this simple practice a try and you might find it to be beneficial for mind, body, and spirit. The insights and methodology of this chapter also fit well in the framework of the practice of the presence of God as explained in chapter 12. Remember that we are holistic beings. Physical action—no matter how ordinary—has spiritual aspects. In the following steps, I am using bread as an example, but you can practice with practically any type of food—as long as you're willing to take things slow.

### HOW TO PRACTICE

1. Bring your attention to the piece of bread. Really see it. Observe its texture, shape, and color. Notice any thoughts that arise in your mind about bread or food in general. Do you have any happy memories associated with bread? Any sad memories?
2. Take some time to smell the bread. What does that smell bring to mind? Any memories? Thoughts? Does the smell cause your mouth to water?
3. Slowly, with attention, bring the bread to your lips and take a bite. Chew slowly, mindfully. Experience the taste of that one bite.
4. When you are ready to swallow, try to feel the bread go down your throat and travel to your stomach. You might even try to imagine that

you are now one bite of bread heavier—or, to put it another way, you have one more little bit of energy to power your body.

5. Ponder how that bite of bread has now become a part of you, strengthening you.

*Note:* As a Christian corollary, you might ponder on the words of Jesus at the Last Supper (as he instituted the Eucharist), "Take. Eat. This is my body."

## VARIATIONS

You can vary this practice in as many different ways as there are kinds of food and situations in which to eat. You might also vary your practice by focusing on a particular sense rather than going through all of them. For instance, how different would your eating be if you focused all day on sight? What about smell? Experiment. Experiment. Experiment.

## COMMON QUESTIONS

**Q:** How slow is too slow to eat in the practice? How fast is too fast to eat in the practice?

**A:** There is no set pace to this practice. It depends on you. While all of us eat more quickly when we are eating mindlessly, our individual pace varies greatly. With that in mind, if your mindful eating practice is moving along so slowly that it begins to impact the rest of your day negatively, then you might consider eating a bit more quickly. You might also consider eating only one meal as a full mindful practice each day and let other meals happen at a more natural pace. It would definitely offer you an interesting contrast. As for eating too fast, we should strive to back off from this end of matters anyway. Mindful eating will always be slower than mindless eating because we're adding time to be grateful. Ponder how much time should be allotted to gratitude; that might help you to find your best pace.

**Q:** Why is it important to view this practice as spiritual instead of physical or biological?

**A:** While there are a host of physical benefits to eating more slowly, that's not the point here. Take time to taste, to enjoy your food. There is no necessary purpose for food to taste good. Ponder a bit on how taste can be a spiritual gift.

Q: Are there some foods or meals that are more important than others for using this practice?

A: Not really. Just listen to common sense. Maybe a quiet dinner at home is a better, or at least easier, place to practice mindful eating than that business lunch with your whole office. If you are eating with your five-year-old . . . well, then, that calls for an entirely different sort of mindfulness. Find your rhythms. Listen to your intuition in developing this practice. Adapt it. Make it your own.

Q: How does this practice connect with a sacramental viewpoint?

A: A sacramental theology is a beautiful foundation for mindful eating. Briefly stated, in a sacramental view, God communicates grace and energy through the physical, created world. With this viewpoint, it is a natural meditation on how matter contains the spirit during mindful eating. While a sacramental view of the world is not necessary to practice mindful eating, in my opinion, it enhances this practice immeasurably.

Q: Should I practice mindful eating in public?

A: It is really up to you. If you are able to take the time, then it might be a good experiment. It might be difficult to concentrate in public. Also, you will find that most public eating is done in a culturally hurried and harried manner (at least in the United States). Mindful eating in public might even be viewed as countercultural. Actually, why not give it a try? Stand out from the crowd.

Q: Could mindful eating be a group practice as well as an individual practice?

A: I view the practice of the Eucharist in churches as a form of group mindful eating (although I think it is more than that too). While it might be a bit more difficult to coordinate as a group, give it a try. As I reiterate over and over, experiment, try, vary your practice. Never be afraid to begin again and again.

Q: What if my mind wanders during the practice, and I begin to eat mindlessly again?

A: You have had a lot of practice in not paying attention while you eat. It will take time to build the habit of consciously eating mindfully; be gentle with yourself. When you realize that your attention has wandered, simply stop, refocus, and start paying attention again, one bite at a time.

## POTENTIAL JOURNALING PROMPTS OR DISCUSSION QUESTIONS

1. What positive experiences did you have while practicing this practice?
2. What negative experiences did you have while practicing this practice?
3. How did you adapt this structure to your situation?
4. Ponder all of the hands that were involved in bringing this morsel of food into your hands: planters, growers, harvesters, manufacturers, packagers, distributors, grocers, etc. Take a moment to thank each one and to write about the chain of support we all need in something as simple as a bite to eat.

# 20

## Drumbeat

### BRIEF BACKGROUND

One of the major pieces in most mindfulness practices is paying attention to our bodies. While most of these activities are concerned with building our attention in stillness, I think it can also be helpful to have some practices that incorporate movement and energy. This practice incorporates music, rhythm, and the release of energy to help us be present in the moment. Have fun with it.

### HOW TO PRACTICE

Make sure you have plenty of room to move with this one.

1. Begin by rooting your feet into the floor. Spread your toes. Find a comfortable standing position because your feet will be the only part of you not moving during this practice.
2. To warm up, take a page from the body scan (chapter 18, page 102) and focus on each body part, starting at the soles of your feet and moving up to the crown of your head. Try to tense that area for one to two breaths, then let go and relax. You should feel warm and relaxed afterward and, perhaps, a bit tingly.
3. Choose some music with a prominent drumbeat. I prefer recordings that are focused on drumbeats without much vocal or orchestral accompaniment. For instance, there are many recordings of Native American drumming or traditional African drumbeats. Find what works for you.
4. While keeping your feet stationary, begin to make small movements in rhythm with the drums. Alternate with moving your legs, arms, shoulders, neck, head, and so on. Remember to keep your feet immobile.

5. Gradually make your rhythmic movements more and more pro-
nounced. Experiment with your tempo, moving slow to fast and back
again. If you are like me, you may be working up quite a sweat in this
process. That's okay. This is definitely a much more active practice than
other mindfulness meditations.

6. At your own pace, or at the end of the music, slowly come to a stop and
take five deep breaths while focusing on feeling all the sensations of
your body right after an intense period of movement.

## VARIATIONS

Variations abound with this practice. You can vary it up with differences in
music. You can experiment with different types of movements, such as swaying, clapping, twisting, turning, bending, stretching, reaching, even shadow
boxing. You don't necessarily need to use a drumbeat. Such a distinctive
rhythm helps in the beginning to focus and synchronize your movements,
especially if you, like me, were tragically born without any sense of internal
rhythm. Try other instruments to see how they strike you. Be imaginative.
This practice is also particularly well-suited to introduce children to mindfulness meditation because it allows for movement and high energy.

## COMMON QUESTIONS

**Q:** Should I do this practice with a group or in public?

**A:** I think this practice has wonderful dimensions when practiced in
a group. If you know some like-minded individuals who want to
experiment, then go for it. As for the general public, it might be a bit
off-putting for you to perform these actions spontaneously in a crowd.
Remember that all mindfulness practices have the intent of building
attention and patient awareness. Practicing your meditations with
onlookers present will tend to offer too many distractions.

**Q:** Is it important to keep my feet immobilized?

**A:** Actually, it is. In this practice, you are learning to balance movement
and stillness in your attention. To keep your feet still will likely go
against your natural inclination. That's good. The unfamiliarity of
movement in this way can help you stay focused.

**Q:** What if I have physical complications that inform against this type of "exercise"?

**A:** Always consult your primary care physician if you suspect any physical activity might be too strenuous for you. With that said, the point of this practice is not really to get exercise or "work up a sweat." I typically do work up a sweat, but it is hardly necessary. You can easily focus on gentle swaying for your movements without attempting anything more strenuous. You will still have access to all of the benefits of the drumbeat practice.

**Q:** Many cultures have ritualistic, rhythmic dancing. Does this practice connect with that idea?

**A:** Absolutely. Moving rhythmically has been a part of religious and spiritual ceremonies since time immemorial. It connects with a deep part of our nature in which our deeply held beliefs require expression in action. This mindfulness practice simply brings the focus to the rhythmic portion of that connection as a way to be present. If your religious tradition contains rhythmic actions, whether they are elaborate symbolic dances or something as simple as genuflection, then you can bring insights from this drumbeat practice to enhance your participation in those ritualistic actions as well.

**Q:** What if I have an intense or mystical experience during this practice?

**A:** Mystical experiences during rhythmic movements are very common. Many religions have noted this feature and developed practices around it. For instance, many Sufi mystics in Islam incorporate whirling movements as part of their meditations. If you have an experience, then write it down. Ponder on it. What insights might you gain, or others gain, through it? However, remember that experience is not the purpose of mindfulness practice. Moment-by-moment awareness and simple presence—actually paying attention to where we are right now—is the main purpose.

**Q:** What if I don't feel that this practice is particularly "spiritual"?

**A:** This is a common question that I get in connection with this practice and other practices that incorporate a high level of physical activity. Just because something is physical does not mean that it is not also spiritual. It is a common misconception that all spiritual and mystical activities require stillness and quiet. While there are many prominent practices centered on peace and quiet, I am deliberately including practices like this one to demonstrate that mystical practices run the gamut of human activity.

## POTENTIAL JOURNALING PROMPTS OR DISCUSSION QUESTIONS

1. What positive experiences did you have while practicing this practice?
2. What negative experiences did you have while practicing this practice?
3. How did you adapt this structure to your situation?
4. What could be the benefits of learning to combine movement (your upper and lower body) with stillness (your feet)?
5. Did anything surprise you in this practice? How? Why?
6. Since we spend so much of our day-to-day life in constant (hurried) motion, how could you take some of the insights from this practice to change your daily routine?

# 21

---

# Fasting

## BRIEF BACKGROUND

Fasting as a mystic practice generally means foregoing food or sleep, also called a "vigil," in order to spend the time otherwise designated for these essential activities in devotion to God for a specified period of time. Within this basic definition, you can fast according to many different versions. Fasting may only result in giving up a particular type of food or certain period of sleep rather than complete abstinence from these activities. Additionally, the reason behind fasting might be individualistic, communal, or part of regular activities within the liturgical year (e.g., Lent). While fasting is not a prayer practice in itself, it has often been coupled with various prayer practices in Christian tradition and various other religious traditions.

Remember: Fasting is a healthy physical practice, but it only becomes a spiritual practice when you are replacing the time you typically spend eating and the dependence we all have, often unconsciously, on food with spiritual seeking. This seeking is usually accomplished by setting these times aside for prayer or meditation, but find your own rhythm here.

## HOW TO PRACTICE

While it may seem simple to say "Don't eat," a successful fast often requires practical steps for implementation.

1. Think of fasting as a skill to be learned at first. You need to ease yourself into it rather than try to go "cold turkey." I highly recommend consulting with your primary care physician before beginning experimentation with fasting.
2. Start with skipping a single meal.

3. As you are able, you might expand your regimen to two meals, three meals, and so on.

4. When you have worked up to fasting an entire day, you may still want to drink fruit juices or other means of nourishment before attempting a water-only fast.

5. You may eventually want to embark on a fast of multiple days. If so, resist the temptation to eat heavier on the days prior to fasting. If anything, try to eat progressively lighter meals to help lessen your appetite.

6. As a last meal before a longer fast, try to eat fresh fruit and vegetables. A similar meal is the best way to break a fast as well, no matter how tempting foods high in sugar or saturated fat might be.

7. Be aware that you will experience significant hunger, weakness, and perhaps dizziness in the first few days of a long fast. Typically, after about three days, you will notice a dramatic shift in your energy levels and hunger pains.

8. You will then experience a period in which you are not "bothered" by the fast as much. This period varies for each individual from a few days to multiple weeks. Once you start to feel hungry again, your body is signaling you that it has used up its reserves, and it is important to begin breaking your fast at this point.

## VARIATIONS

### Daniel Fast

One of the more popular versions of a partial fast is to fast for a lengthy period, typically forty days, such as the fast of the prophet Daniel (see Dan. 1:11–20). Essentially, during this time, you would only eat fresh fruit and vegetables and drink only water. This variation is a good way to ease into fasting, but it does not focus as much on setting aside certain times for prayer and meditation as other variations.

### Activities

Throughout history, abstinence from particular activities has been used as a means to focus on God or the divine. These activities have constituted a diverse range from watching television to sexual intercourse. Use your imagination, and think of what activities might be coming between you and your own spiritual search.

## Speech

This variation is typically utilized as a vow of silence in various monastic traditions. A vow of silence may not be as realistic in the work-a-day world, but you could fast from certain kinds of speech. I have known participants to fast from gossip or from foul language.

## Sleep

As noted above, fasting from sleep is typically called a vigil or "keeping vigil." For many, this variation is one of the few versions that is actually more challenging than abstinence from food. For obvious reasons, fasting from sleep must only be attempted in short duration. It is more common to incorporate an element of this type of fasting by rising early or staying up late in order to have some uninterrupted time in prayer or meditation.

## Fasting by Addition

Fasting is often conceived of only in terms of "subtraction," by answering, "What can I take out of my life to focus more on God or the divine?" What about experimenting with fasting through addition? Don't just take away a particular activity; consciously add a specific activity. For instance, rather than skipping a meal, try adding the activity of volunteering at a soup kitchen. You might end up skipping a meal as a result, but you might find an enriching shift in perspective by focusing on what you can give rather than just on what you can deny yourself.

## COMMON QUESTIONS

**Q:** Is it really so important to talk to my doctor?

**A:** Yes, it is. While fasting is healthy for our bodies in an ideal sense, there are many health situations that preclude fasting. Check with your doctor, and take things slowly. Better to be safe than sorry.

**Q:** Why is it so hard to find instructions on how to fast?

**A:** Up until modern times, fasting was such a common practice that most spiritual authors did not think it was necessary to write out steps on how to implement it. They assumed that anyone attempting to fast could always go to their priest or other spiritual guide.

**Q:** Is there a biblical precedent for when to fast?

**A:** Fasts are often connected to prayer in the Bible, particularly prayer with the express purpose of seeking God's will on a proper course of action. There is also some biblical (and nearly biblical) precedent for fasting on particular days. For instance, the *Didache,* an early Christian compilation of teachings of the apostles, enjoins the faithful to fast on Wednesdays and Fridays primarily because Jews in the same era fasted on Tuesdays and Thursdays. While it is helpful to have a regular day to fast when developing fasting as a skill, that is a guideline, not a rule.

**Q:** Does fasting make prayer more effective?

**A:** It depends on what you mean by effective. If you mean that fasting makes it more likely that God will do whatever you want, then no—emphatically no. You may notice from comments I have made concerning other practices that many practices have the aim of quieting us down in order to pay attention to what God has been showing us all along. Think of the effectiveness of fasting in that context. Fasting does not get God on our "side," but it does help to clear away the distractions in our lives and priorities so we can more clearly see what God has been doing all the while.

**Q:** What should I do if I end up thinking only about food for the entire fast?

**A:** This is a very common question. Some practitioners find that they have to avoid food entirely in order to keep it out of their minds. If that is a possible course of action, you might see how it works for you. However, if you find after multiple attempts that you cannot concentrate on anything other than food, then this practice may not be the most suitable one for you. I would encourage you not to throw out fasting entirely; rather, focus on using one of the variations of partial fasting or alternate fasting. Remember, fasting, like all of these spiritual practices, are not matters of success and failure. You are experimenting to find out what is helpful for you and what is less than helpful.

**Q:** What about communal fasting?

**A:** Communal fasting has a rich history in many religious traditions. Few activities are as tangibly unifying as the communal experience of fasting. Such fasting often follows a specific religious season, but religious groups may also have "called fasts" during which all members fast together to seek some spiritual truth, social justice action, or the will of God. The concept of a "hunger strike" is similar, but a hunger strike is a typically a political rather than religious tool.

**Q:** What about Lent? What about Ramadan?

**A:** Lent is the Christian season of fasting and repentance that leads up to the celebration of Christ's death and resurrection during the season of Easter. It is a forty-day fast, and it is often celebrated as a partial fast. The strictest requirements for Lenten fasts are found in Eastern Orthodox Christianity, but Lenten fasts and observances are also integral to Episcopal/Anglican and Roman Catholic spiritual traditions. Ramadan is the month of fasting that is practiced in many variants of Islam. This fast is a total fast during the daylight hours with some simple food eaten at night, which is likely adapted from the Eastern Orthodox model. These fasting seasons in both Christian and Islamic tradition are voluntary, but there may be strong communal encouragement to participate.

**Q:** Should I tell other people that I am fasting?

**A:** That depends entirely on the type of fast, your reasons for fasting, and your personal preference. There is biblical precedent for fasting without calling attention to yourself (see Matt. 6:16–18), but these instructions do seem to refer to fasting that is solely done for the purposes of social standing, which could only occur in a society in which fasting was common.

## POTENTIAL JOURNALING PROMPTS /DISCUSSION QUESTIONS

1. What positive experiences did you have while practicing this practice?
2. What negative experiences did you have while practicing this practice?
3. How did you adapt this structure to your situation?
4. How did you meet God in this practice?
5. How did fasting help you pay attention?
6. What about the fasting experience surprised you?

# 22

---

# Labyrinths

## BRIEF BACKGROUND

The use of labyrinths for multiple purposes, both spiritual and secular, dates back beyond the beginnings of the Christian tradition. However, Christians have utilized labyrinths as aids to prayer for centuries and in various contexts. As a mystic practice, you may walk the labyrinth while praying and meditating on certain aspects of God, spiritual needs, or difficult questions. Occasionally, you might also want to pause at the center of the labyrinth for a time of prayer and reflection. While the focus is on prayer, the activity of walking is a simple but effective means to focus your attention much like how repetitious words are used in centering prayer and the Jesus Prayer.

## HOW TO PRACTICE

Remember that labyrinths are not mazes. There are not wrong turns or false leads. There is only one winding path from the point of entry to the center. You go in to the labyrinth in the same way you will leave it.

1. Set aside a time for walking a labyrinth. Plan to walk much more slowly than normal, so allow at least fifteen to thirty minutes for your first time. You will find your own rhythm as you go.
2. Begin to walk slowly and deliberately.
3. As you walk, decide where to fix your gaze. Will you look at your feet? straight ahead? at the center? Experiment with where you look and what that intention symbolizes for you.
4. As you walk, pray. There are no rules for how to pray. You might be asking for help or guidance. You might not have any particular intention other than walking with God. You might pray aloud or silently. You might pray as you walk or stop for a few moments at

different intervals in the labyrinth. Finding your own rhythm is part of the practice.

5. At the center, plan to spend a bit more time than elsewhere. Ponder the center of your life as you stand or sit in the center of the labyrinth. Perhaps offer a prayer of thanksgiving for the way you have been led so far.

6. As you follow the path back, pray and ponder some more. You might ponder whether you are retracing your steps or if this might be a new path for you. Ponder the difference between the path you can see (i.e., the labyrinth) and the path you cannot see (i.e., the direction of your life). Pray and ponder as you feel motivated.

7. When you arrive back at the point of entry, stop for a moment. Take a few deep breaths. Ponder whether the path really ends when you step out of the labyrinth.

8. Walk back into the press of daily life.

## VARIATIONS

Labyrinths offer endless variations for construction ranging from the simple to elaborate and from the temporary to the permanent. On one end of the spectrum, you can create a labyrinth by arranging stones in a labyrinth pattern or even using tape on carpet. On the other end of the spectrum, some ancient churches have beautifully crafted permanent labyrinths constructed right into the floor. Typically, labyrinths follow the cross-pattern or the rose-pattern as seen in the pictures below:

Cross-Pattern Labyrinth

Rose-Pattern Labyrinth

However, as with all of these practices, experiment and be creative. I have even used a computer printout of a labyrinth which I "walked" with my fingers while praying, and my wife has sculpted finger labyrinths out of clay.

## COMMON QUESTIONS

**Q:** Is there a right way to walk a labyrinth?

**A:** It depends on who you talk to, but I advocate that there is no one right way or wrong way to walk a labyrinth. You might even try walking it backwards if you like. It certainly would make me pay attention.

**Q:** Is there any difference between a labyrinth and a maze?

**A:** Yes, labyrinths only have one path without any blind alleys or false leads. Mazes have dead ends of all sorts.

**Q:** Is there any difference between a labyrinth and a prayer walk?

**A:** Technically, you are going through the same motions, yet labyrinths and prayer walks are often used for different purposes. Labyrinths tend to be used for centering, reflection, and looking within oneself. Prayer walks tend to be associated with intercessory prayer or prayer focused on a particular outcome. However, these are only general distinctions. If you do not have access to a labyrinth or the necessary tools to make one, then you can simply walk in any path or direction with an inward intention of moving toward your center. Do not let the lack of an outer apparatus be a reason for not experimenting with a practice.

**Q:** What if I can't find a labyrinth near me?

**A:** If you can't find a labyrinth, then you can easily make one of stones outdoors or tape on carpet indoors. You can even draw or print one on paper and "walk" the labyrinth with your fingers. Using an Internet search engine, you can type "finger labyrinth" and find numerous options to buy or print one.

**Q:** Should walking a labyrinth be an individual or group practice?

**A:** Both. Multiple individuals use outdoor and church labyrinths at the same time. Groups can also use them together by stopping at certain points for a communal prayer. If you have access to, or want to form, a labyrinth group, then I would encourage you to experiment with group labyrinth practice. See if you prefer walking the path in a group or by yourself. You might even find you prefer walking alone or with others at different times in your life.

**Q:** Where did labyrinths come from originally?

**A:** Some of the books on the list of "Resources for Further Study" on page 224 delve deeply into this question. Labyrinths date far back in human history and have been used by many different religions. The use of the labyrinth came most directly into the Christian tradition through the Celtic people.

**Q:** What about using a labyrinth for meditation rather than prayer?

**A:** It is perfectly fine to focus on meditation rather than prayer while walking the labyrinth. However, as you may notice from other chapters, the lines between meditation and prayer are quite fuzzy with regard to spiritual practices anyway. I only use prayer terminology here because labyrinths have historically been connected with a conversation framework or the context of "walking with God." If such imagery is not helpful for you, then please feel free to disregard or reinterpret it.

**Q:** What about using poetry or song in a labyrinth?

**A:** I have not personally used either poetry or song in walking a labyrinth. However, there is nothing to preclude such a practice, particularly if you are walking the labyrinth by yourself and would not intrude on anyone's thoughts by "bursting into song." Try it out. See how it strikes you.

## POTENTIAL JOURNALING PROMPTS OR DISCUSSION QUESTIONS

1. What positive experiences did you have while practicing this practice?
2. What negative experiences did you have while practicing this practice?
3. How did you adapt this structure to your situation?
4. How did you meet God in this practice?
5. How did walking help you pay attention?
6. What about the labyrinth experience surprised you?

# 23

## Pilgrimage

### BRIEF BACKGROUND

Pilgrimage is a little bit more than travel or tourism. Historically, if you wanted to "go on pilgrimage," then you were looking for two essential components. First, you, as a pilgrim, would have been seeking to travel to a holy site, which was often a great distance away. What constitutes a holy site? Sites became sacred when an important event in the history of a particular religion happened at that place. For instance, the Church of the Holy Sepulchre was built on the spot where Jesus of Nazareth was crucified according to tradition, and it has been a consistent place for Christian pilgrimage since at least the fourth century. The second necessary component of pilgrimage is your attitude. The intention of each pilgrim sets the tone for travel to the holy site for spiritual purposes in order to worship. Attitude and intention set a far different tone for pilgrimage than for religious tourism. Often, practices of (limited) fasting and prayer are coupled with pilgrimage in the course of the journey.

### HOW TO PRACTICE

1. The first step for pilgrimage is often the most overlooked one: unrest. The sense or feeling of calling to go on a pilgrimage begins quietly and almost invisibly, but it begins with a persistent sense of disquiet and restlessness. Unrest is connected to simple wanderlust, but it is more intangible. You do not just have the hunger to see new places; you have the hunger to see with new eyes.

2. From that point, you begin the work of preparation. Preparing for pilgrimage includes all of the natural steps in getting ready for a big

trip—maps, arrangements, and organization—but you are also preparing your soul for the road. If you plan to walk a traditional pilgrimage, you will also need to prepare physically for such extended walking. At this point, you will want to read books of devotion and holiness. You may fast. You will most definitely pray. Without a soul prepared for the road, you are just going on a trip, so don't rush this step.

3. Go. Walk. Enter onto the pilgrim way.

4. Stop often and at important sites and intervals to pray and meditate.

5. Consider keeping a journal of your experiences. Many pilgrim journals have been written by the wanderers of the ages. Join your voice to theirs.

6. Once you reach your destination, plan to spend considerable time in prayer and meditation. Like the step of preparation, don't rush. Reaching your destination is less like crossing a finish line and more like acclimating to a high altitude. Give your body (and soul) time to adjust.

7. Return. When you return, don't be too alarmed if your day-to-day routine seems disorienting, perhaps even disheartening. After all, you are a different person. You are seeing your world with new eyes. Maybe the pilgrimage has many lessons for you to implement to change your old life once you return.

8. Wait. The journey does lead us back, but it often plants a permanent seed of disquiet, of need, to visit the sacred places, to commune with the holy. You might find yourself called back to the road. Who knows?

## VARIATIONS

Pilgrimage is infinitely variable by place and by individual. Each person may even perform the same pilgrimage in different ways. I recommend that you not define pilgrimage too narrowly. Can a camping trip to the mountains become a pilgrimage? What about a long car ride? While destination definitely plays an essential role in traditional concepts of pilgrimage, the most important piece is intention. Religious tourism and retreats are different, but there are points of contact for them with pilgrimage. More than with any other practice, on pilgrimage you only take what you bring with you.

# COMMON QUESTIONS

**Q:** Is it enough of a "call" to pilgrimage to want to go on one?

**A:** The "call" of the pilgrim is an individualized one, so it can "look" like a simple want to go on one at the beginning. The only caution I offer is that such initial curiosity should deepen before you actually decide to go on a pilgrimage. A pilgrimage can be a weighty undertaking, so you don't want to just head off on a whim.

**Q:** How long should the preparation phase last?

**A:** It should last longer than the preparation for a typical trip because you need to do all the necessary arrangements for a typical trip and do the harder work of soul preparation. That doesn't mean that your soul has to be "in order" before you set out, but it does mean that you have taken quite a bit of time to sit with the purpose of the trip as spiritual.

**Q:** What about pilgrim companions?

**A:** Companions on a pilgrimage are quite common. While in some sense every person does a pilgrimage on her or his own, companions are often welcome and, indeed, part of the way God speaks to us when we go on pilgrimage. Additionally, if you plan to go to one of the recognized pilgrimage sites for any major religion, then you'll find that fellow travelers are unavoidable.

**Q:** Does pilgrimage have to lead to a traditional holy site?

**A:** No, but there is a reason that traditional holy sites are often the sites of pilgrimage. These are the places that historically have been eye-opening and perspective-changing. Pilgrimage can lead anywhere that is deeply spiritual and meaningful to you, but that meaning may be communal as well as individual.

**Q:** How long should a pilgrimage be?

**A:** There is no set length, although I do offer the advice that if you are thinking about pilgrimage solely in terms of "minimum requirements," then that's a clue that you need to spend more time in the preparation phase.

**Q:** Do you have to "walk" a pilgrimage rather than other forms of transportation?

A: Walking, usually over the course of many days, is the traditional method for going on pilgrimage; however, there may be extenuating circumstances, so don't feel that walking is the only element to a pilgrimage. Also, as with any major physical activity or exertion, you may want to consult with your physician before attempting the physical rigors of the pilgrimage.

Q: What about a tour of religious sites? Does that "count" as pilgrimage?

A: Well, I don't think "counting" is really the way to approach pilgrimage. With that said, most religious tours are not set up to be particularly conducive to the meditative aspects of a full pilgrimage. Be aware that the religious tour has a more informative and academic purpose rather than a contemplative purpose. There is some overlap, but don't get caught in the trap of trying to fit a square peg into a round hole.

Q: What about retreats and religious camps? Do they "count" as pilgrimage?

A: See the above comment about "counting" because it applies here too. However, retreats and religious camps do tend to have a contemplative purpose, so they tread more of the same spiritual ground as pilgrimage. The element of journey may be missing, but these retreats and camps often take place in beautiful, natural settings. Also, for the religious traditions in which pilgrimage has been less emphasized, retreats offer the closest parallel.

Q: What if I don't feel anything when I reach my destination?

A: This is a very common experience. There is a lot of emotional impact and build-up from the journey itself so reaching the destination may seem like something of a let-down. In recognition of this possibility, I recommend staying at the destination as long as possible in order to let the full impact sink into your being. However, remember that a particular feeling is not the point of a pilgrimage. The point of a pilgrimage is a new perspective. You may not feel anything because you don't know how to feel in this new context, this new perspective. Give it time, and don't load yourself up with unrealistic expectations.

## POTENTIAL JOURNALING PROMPTS
## OR DISCUSSION QUESTIONS

1. What positive experiences did you have while practicing this practice?
2. What negative experiences did you have while practicing this practice?
3. How did you adapt this structure to your situation?
4. How did you meet God in this practice?
5. How did pilgrimage change your perspective?
6. What about pilgrimage surprised you?

# Section 5

# EMBODYING

Almost fifteen years ago, I was researching for my master's thesis in Christian theology. At the time, I was considering many avenues for writing, and one of those avenues was the growing popularity of "spiritual formation," as it was then called, among "cutting edge" evangelical churches (the churches which became known as the emergent church). I serendipitously picked up a volume by one of the prominent voices in the movement, Doug Pagitt, and turned to a chapter detailing the use of yoga in his church.[1] In the course of the chapter, Pagitt quoted the comments of several of his parishioners. Many of them noted the value of yoga practices in bringing a physical dimension to their spirituality because Christianity did not have a physical component. I had an immediate, visceral reaction to that conclusion. I thought, "How dare they say that Christianity doesn't have a physical component!" So I started my research into detailing and describing all of the physical components of spirituality that Christianity actually has.

After a lot of time to research, think, and put everything in context, I did find some important issues for Christian spirituality and mysticism in general. First, Christians *do* have mystic practices that qualify as physical, but these practices are generally of a negative cast. In other words, Christian practices of the body tend to focus on depriving the body of something, like in fasting. Also, physically active practices tend to focus on a spiritual purpose behind a mundane activity, such as walking in the use of labyrinths and going on a pilgrimage.

Christian spirituality has physical activity, but that doesn't mean there is nothing to learn from other religious traditions concerning the totality of physical experience. Second, Christianity has fought off and on for its entire history with the concept that the physical is bad or at least "lesser,"

---

1. Doug Pagitt, *Reimagining Spiritual Formation: A Week in the Life of an Experimental Church* (Grand Rapids, MI: Zondervan, 2005), 67–84.

and the spiritual is good or "better." It is a pervasive issue in popular con-
ceptions of Christianity. The point that bothered me in Pagitt's book has
some truth to it even if it is not entirely consistent with the facts. Third, and
most importantly, here is a golden opportunity for spiritual borrowing.

As you may have noticed from the earlier sections of the book, many
practices of the Christian tradition have tremendous worth in connecting
with God. So much development in this direction was possible because
Christians have always viewed the process of detachment as only part of
the mystic journey. They say so much about contemplation—or enlightenment—because Christians believe that the most important part of
their spirituality is what one does after that enlightenment/contemplation
occurs. Now, on the other side of the fence, other religious traditions have
developed more nuanced practices for a spirituality of the body.

The practical upshot for those of us who are ready to "just begin" with
spiritual practices is that we can pull from multiple traditions to experiment. As we move into this section, I will offer some practices that are
based on Pilates and yoga, but I am blending them with mindfulness meditations and centering prayer. I am not limiting this book to any one tradition; however, I do pull quite a bit from Christianity since that is my own
perspective. In light of this cross-fertilization, I am going to approach some
of these practices in a new way. I will present the practices of the body that
arise from Pilates and yoga, but I will offer Christian theological reflections
to go with the poses and movements. My advice is to take this method, if
you wish, and apply it in reverse to the practices from earlier sections to see
how Christian practices can also be borrowed by other religions and rein-
terpreted into the context of those traditions. Feel free to experiment with
all of these practices no matter what your religious or spiritual background
may be. So let's start trying something new . . .

# 24

## Body Flow:
## Pilates with Mindfulness

### BRIEF BACKGROUND

Many of the previous practices of the body focus on self-denial or simple forms of physical activity, such as walking; now I want to propose something a little more vigorous. By "body flow," I mean a series of specific exercises or poses that a practitioner will move through in an unbroken sequence, moving directly from one to the next. As with any exercise routine, please consult with your primary care physician if you have any reservations about the level of exertion or any physical limitations that you may have. With that caveat in mind, I would like to introduce you to a combination of practices: the exercise routines developed by Joseph Pilates and mindfulness meditation.

Mindfulness meditation is not all of one type, as you saw in my earlier treatments of practices arising from that framework. However, all mindfulness exercises have a common goal of being fully present in each moment of daily life. This awareness of presence is often achieved through very simple concentration exercises on your breath (as in the sitting meditation) or on the sensations that your body provides to you (as in the body scan). It is that concentrated sense of being present right here, right now, which I encourage you to bring to the flow of bodily exercises coming from Pilates.

Joseph Pilates was a pioneer of rehabilitation and the developing "physical culture" of the early twentieth century. He first began developing the series of exercises that bear his name in response to the poor posture, incomplete recovery, and general ill health of soldiers returning from the trenches of World War I. Eventually, he would incorporate a series of thirty-four mat exercises, which he presented in the book *Return to Life through Contrology* (1945). Contrology was Pilates' original name for his exercise system, but it proved much easier to refer to these exercises by the founder's name. The exercises that I incorporate in this body flow are pulled from Pilates' original thirty-four, and I refer to his descriptions in how to perform them. There are many, many variations and routines based on Pilates' original series; do not feel limited to the three series that I suggest. Experiment with other methods too. Mindfulness and Pilates' exercises pair particularly well because Pilates exercises—as originally proposed by Joseph Pilates—focused much more on the aspect of body control than physical exertion or strength training. At each point in the body flow, maintaining your awareness in the present moment is far more important than perfect performance or number of repetitions. Do not sacrifice inner focus for outer achievement.

## HOW TO PRACTICE: BEGINNER SERIES

### Practice 1: The Hundred

1. Lie flat on the mat or floor with your arms resting at your sides and palms on the floor. Breathe deeply for five breaths, feeling the sensations of your body resting on the floor or mat.

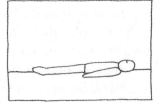

2. Bring your attention to your core, your belly button, and concentrate on tensing your abdominal muscles. Focus on making your core feel solid and stable. Imagine your belly button rooted down into your spine. Throughout this flow, you will concentrate your attention on your core in this way.

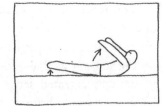

3. As you inhale, raise your feet about two inches off the mat, and raise your arms about six inches above the rest of your body. Remember to focus on the stability of your core during these motions.

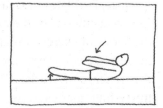

4. As you exhale, move your arms down to your thighs and back up to about six inches

above your body five times. Feel the movement of air in your hands and fingertips as
you do so.

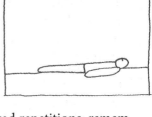

5. As you inhale, move your arms down and
   up in the same way for a count of five.

6. Repeat this alternation of exhaling and
   inhaling, ten times or for a total of one hundred repetitions, remembering to keep your core stable and steady throughout the exercise.

7. Relax completely. Perhaps stretch your arms and legs as far as you can in
   opposite directions to stretch out your core after all that work. Breathe
   deeply for five breaths, feeling the sensations of the floor against your
   skin and the air as you breathe it into your lungs and out again.

## Practice 2: The Roll Up

1. Lie flat on the mat or floor with your arms resting at your sides and
   palms on the floor. Breathe deeply for five breaths, feeling the sensations
   of your body resting on the floor or mat.

2. Bring your arms and hands up, first to a
   ninety-degree angle, then to rest on the
   floor stretched out above your head with
   palms up.

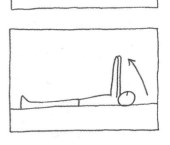

3. Bring your attention to your core, your
   belly button, and concentrate on tensing
   your abdominal muscles. Focus on making
   your core feel solid and stable. Imagine
   your belly button rooted down into your
   spine. Throughout this flow, you will
   concentrate your attention on your core in
   this way.

4. As you slowly bring your arms back up, roll
   up with your core to a seated position.

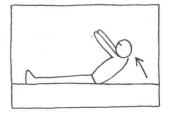

5. Then continue, reaching forward with your
   arms, stretching to touch your toes. Move
   slowly, mindfully, remembering to breathe
   deeply, inhaling and exhaling as you go.

Move fluidly. Do not "jerk" yourself up or try to "bounce" forward to touch your toes. The flow is more important than the end result.

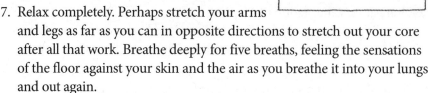

6. Repeat the roll up five more times.

7. Relax completely. Perhaps stretch your arms and legs as far as you can in opposite directions to stretch out your core after all that work. Breathe deeply for five breaths, feeling the sensations of the floor against your skin and the air as you breathe it into your lungs and out again.

## Practice 3: The One Leg Circle

1. Lie flat on the mat or floor with your arms resting at your sides and palms on the floor. Breathe deeply for five breaths, feeling the sensations of your body resting on the floor or mat.

2. Bring your attention to your core, your belly button, and concentrate on tensing your abdominal muscles. Focus on making your core feel solid and stable. Imagine your belly button rooted down into your spine. Throughout this flow, you will concentrate your attention on your core in this way.

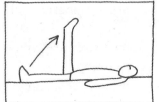

3. Slowly raise your right leg to a ninety-degree angle. Keep the leg straight, or you can have a slight bend in your leg for flexibility issues. Do not arch your back throughout this flow. Keep it rooted to the floor. Perhaps mindfully imagine roots attaching from your back to the floor like a tree, stabilizing your core stomach and back areas.

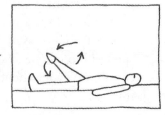

4. Slowly move your leg in a clockwise direction for three full rotations; breathe deeply as you proceed.

5. Slowly move your leg in a counterclockwise direction for three full rotations; once again, breathe deeply as you proceed.

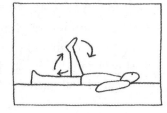

6. Repeat this flow with your left leg.

7. Relax completely. Perhaps stretch your arms and legs as far as you can in opposite directions to stretch out your core after all that work. Breathe deeply for five breaths, feeling the sensations of the floor against your skin and the air as you breathe it into your lungs and out again.

## Practice 4: The One Leg Stretch

1. Lie flat on the mat or floor with your arms resting at your sides and palms on the floor. Breathe deeply for five breaths, feeling the sensations of your body resting on the floor or mat.

2. Bring your attention to your core, your belly button, and concentrate on tensing your abdominal muscles. Focus on making your core feel solid and stable. Imagine your belly button rooted down into your spine. Throughout this flow, you will concentrate your attention on your core in this way.

3. Mindfully draw your head up and forward until your chin touches your chest, raising your shoulders slightly off the floor or mat. You will maintain this position of head and shoulders throughout this practice.

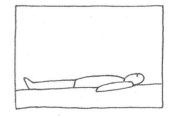

4. As you inhale, bend your right leg and draw your knee up toward your nose as far as you can. Place your hands on your shin below your knee in order to maintain stability in this part of the practice.

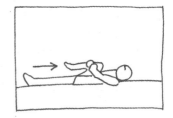

5. As you exhale, stretch your right leg back to its full length.

6. Repeat this process with your left leg.

7. Complete five repetitions with both legs. Don't forget to coordinate the movement of your legs with the inhalation and exhalation of your breath.

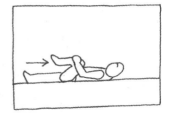

8. Relax completely. Perhaps stretch your arms and legs as far as you can in opposite directions to stretch out your core after all that work. Breathe deeply for five breaths, feeling the sensations of the floor against your skin and the air as you breathe it into your lungs and out again.

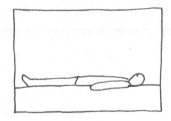

## Practice 5: The Spine Stretch

1. Sit up straight on the mat or floor with your legs stretched out in front of you and with your arms resting at your sides with palms up. Breathe deeply for five breaths, feeling the sensations of your body resting on the floor or mat.

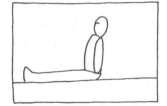

2. Bring your attention to your core, your belly button, and concentrate on tensing your abdominal muscles. Focus on making your core feel solid and stable. Imagine your belly button rooted down into your spine. Throughout this flow, you will concentrate your attention on your core in this way.

3. Draw your chin down to your chest and roll forward to touch your toes. Hold at the point of stretch, not strain. It is not important whether you touch your toes or not; rather, hold the tension at the moment of stretch and breathe at that point, in and out, for a count of five.

4. Slowly come back up to the starting position and end the practice with five more deep breaths. Be mindful of the air as it enters your nostrils, moves down to your lungs, and back out again through exhalation.

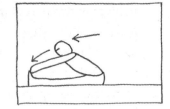

## Practice 6: The Saw

1. Sit up straight on the mat or floor with your legs spread out as wide as possible and with your arms stretched out on either side at shoulder height. Breathe deeply for five breaths, feeling the sensations of your legs resting on the floor or mat and the sensations of your arms as you hold them out.

2. Bring your attention to your core, your belly button, and concentrate on tensing your abdominal muscles. Focus on making your core feel solid and stable. Imagine your belly button rooted down into your spine. Throughout this flow, you will concentrate your attention on your core in this way.

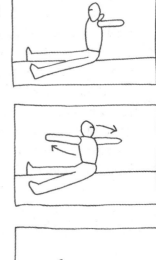

3. Slowly reach your right arm toward your left foot, stretching forward from your waist as you go. Hold at the point of stretch, not strain. It is not important whether you touch your toes or not; rather, hold the tension at the moment of stretch and breathe at that point, in and out, for a count of five.

4. Repeat this motion with your left arm and your right foot.

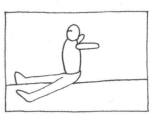

5. Slowly come back up to the starting position and end the practice with five more deep breaths. Be mindful of the air as it enters your nostrils, moves down to your lungs, and back out again through exhalation.

## Practice 7: The Double Leg Kick

1. Lie facedown on the mat or floor with your head resting on your hands. Breathe deeply for five breaths, feeling the sensations of your body resting on the floor or mat.

2. Bring your attention to your core, your belly button, and concentrate on tensing your abdominal muscles. Focus on making your core feel solid and stable. Imagine your belly button rooted down into your spine. Throughout this flow, you will concentrate your attention on your core in this way.

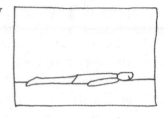

3. Slowly bend your legs at the knee, and gently kick your feet backward (toward your head) three times. Only bend your legs at the knee for this portion of the practice.

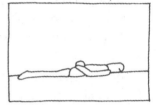

4. Stretch your legs back out and hold them two inches off the floor. Meanwhile, interlace your fingers and stretch your arms back behind you to lift your face and shoulders off the mat or floor and back toward your feet.

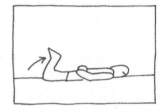

5. Hold this position for one long, deep inhalation and exhalation and then return to the starting position in step one.

6. Complete the circuit of this practice five times. Remember to focus on the stability of your core and the flow of the movement. It is not about working up a sweat; it is about being fully present in the moment.

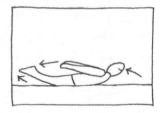

## Practice 8: The Scissors

1. Lie flat on the mat or floor with your arms resting at your sides and palms on the floor. Breathe deeply for five breaths, feeling the sensations of your body resting on the floor or mat.

2. Bring your attention to your core, your belly button, and concentrate on tensing your abdominal muscles. Focus on making your core feel solid and stable. Imagine your belly button rooted down into your spine. Throughout this flow, you will concentrate your attention on your core in this way.

3. Draw your straight legs up until your body rests on your head, neck, shoulders, upper arms, and elbows. Imagine making a "C" with your body where your feet are at the top of the letter and your head is at the bottom. Take a moment or two to breathe deeply and stabilize your balance at this position in the practice.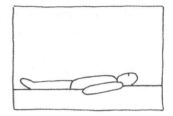

4. Split your legs in opposite directions, while keeping them both straight at the knee. Your right leg will "scissor" toward your head, and your left leg will "scissor" away from your head. Take a moment when your legs are as far apart as possible to feel the stretch between them for one deep inhalation and exhalation.

5. Switch legs with your left leg moving toward your head and your right leg moving away from your head.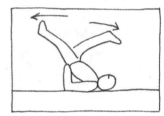

6. Complete this scissoring motion with your legs five times. Remember to focus on the stability of your core and the flow of the movement. It is not about working up a sweat; it is about being fully present in the moment.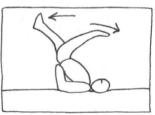

7. This practice may be more difficult than the previous ones, so you might take an extra moment of pause to stretch out and relax your body. Find the rhythm of your breathing again. Concentrate on the sensations of your body and let them root you in the present moment.

## Practice 9: The Bicycle

1. Lie flat on the mat or floor with your arms resting at your sides and palms on the floor. Breathe deeply for five breaths, feeling the sensations of your body resting on the floor or mat.

2. Bring your attention to your core, your belly button, and concentrate on tensing your abdominal muscles. Focus on making your core feel solid and stable. Imagine your belly button rooted down into your spine. Throughout this flow, you will concentrate your attention on your core in this way.

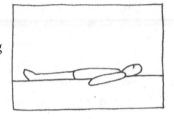

3. Draw your straight legs up until your body rests on your head, neck, shoulders, upper arms, and elbows. Imagine making a "C" with your body where your feet are at the top of the letter and your head is at the bottom. Take a moment or two to breathe deeply and stabilize your balance at this position in the practice.

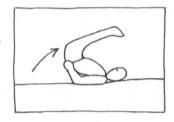

4. Split your legs in opposite directions, and bend each leg at the knee. Imagine yourself to be pedaling an imaginary upside-down bicycle in this fashion. Don't rush through your pedaling. Go as slowly as you can while maintaining your balance so you can concentrate on feeling each movement and being present in it.

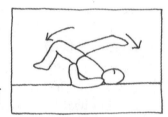

5. Resist the temptation to relax your core in this practice. Your core is keeping your balance in this movement, especially if you are concentrated on pedaling slowly. Your core is the seat of your balance and the place of rest for your spirit. If you increase speed and move away from this point of balance, then you will also increase anxiety and a feeling of rootlessness.

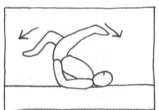

6. Complete ten full cycles with your "bicycle." Then, very slowly, return to lying flat and still on your mat or floor. End the practice with five more deep breaths. Be mindful of the air as it enters your nostrils, moves down to your lungs, and back out again through exhalation.

## Practice 10: The Side Kick

1. Lie resting on your right side on the mat or floor with your arms crossed behind your head with your fingers interlaced. Breathe deeply for five breaths, feeling the sensations of your body resting on the floor or mat.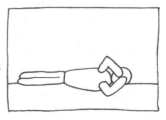

2. Bring your attention to your core, your belly button, and concentrate on tensing your abdominal muscles. Focus on making your core feel solid and stable. Imagine your belly button rooted down into your spine. Throughout this flow, you will concentrate your attention on your core in this way.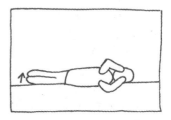

3. With control, swing your left ("top") leg forward to a ninety-degree angle in front of you. Try not to move your torso or hips as you swing your leg. Take a deep inhalation and exhalation as you hold this position.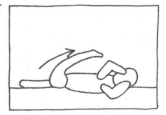

4. Then, with control, swing your left ("top") leg backward as far as you can and hold. Again, try not to move your torso or hips as you swing your leg. Take a deep inhalation and exhalation as you hold this position.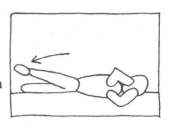

5. Repeat this whole circuit five times, then turn over to lie on your left side with right leg on top. Complete five circuits with this leg.

6. Slowly come back up to the starting position and end the practice with five more deep breaths. Be mindful of the air as it enters your nostrils, moves down to your lungs, and back out again through exhalation.

## Practice 11: The Push-Up

This practice is likely the single most physically taxing practice of this body flow, so go easy on yourself and focus on maintaining good form throughout.

1. Stand up straight on the mat or floor with your arms resting at your sides. Breathe deeply for five breaths, feeling the sensations of the bottoms of your feet resting on the floor or mat and the sensations of your arms as you rest them against your body.

2. Bring your attention to your core, your belly button, and concentrate on tensing your abdominal muscles. Focus on making your core feel solid and stable. Imagine your belly button rooted down into your spine. Throughout this flow, you will concentrate your attention on your core in this way.

3. Slowly roll down to touch your toes while keeping your knees as straight as possible. Take one slow, deep breath to be mindful at this point.

4. Proceed slowly to "walk" your hands forward on the floor or mat until you are arched in a pose resembling a triangle or "downward facing dog" from yoga. Take one slow, deep breath again to be mindful. Feel the stretch of your body. Right here, right now.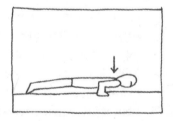

5. Continue to "walk" your hands forward until you are in the traditional push-up position. Keep your elbows close to your body as you enter this phase of the practice. Press down and up five times slowly and mindfully, coordinating with your breathing. Inhale as you lower yourself toward the ground; exhale as you push your arms back up to full length.

6. Take five long, deep inhalations and exhalations at this point, then "walk" your hands back up to the point of touching your toes, and then slowly round back up to the beginning point of the practice.

## Practice 12: The Spine Twist

1. Sit up straight on the mat or floor with your legs straight out in front of you and with your arms stretched out on either side at shoulder height. Breathe deeply for five breaths, feeling the sensations of your legs resting on the floor or mat and the sensations of your arms as you hold them out.

2. Bring your attention to your core, your belly button, and concentrate on tensing your abdominal muscles. Focus on making your core feel solid and stable. Imagine your belly button rooted down into your spine. Throughout this flow, you will concentrate your attention on your core in this way.

3. While keeping your legs and head motionless, twist your arms to the right as far as you can go to feel a stretch, not strain, and hold that position. Slowly inhale and exhale three breaths, and concentrate on feeling these breaths go through the twist, opening up any place of tension in your muscles.

4. Repeat this twist to the left. Hold for three breaths.

5. Slowly come back up to the starting position and end the practice with five more deep breaths. Be mindful of the air as it enters your nostrils, moves down to your lungs, and back out again through exhalation.

# HOW TO PRACTICE: INTERMEDIATE SERIES

## Practice 1: The Rolling Back

1. While sitting up on a mat, bend your knees and draw your legs to your chest. Bend forward to grab your ankles firmly. It may help to cross your grip, grabbing your left ankle with your right hand and vice versa.

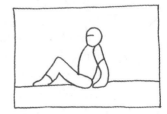

2. Bring your attention to your core, your belly button, and concentrate on tensing your abdominal muscles. Focus on making your core feel solid and stable. Imagine your belly button rooted down into your spine. Throughout this flow, you will concentrate your attention on your core in this way.

3. Breathe in deeply, mindfully, and concentrate on rocking yourself back by drawing your belly button further back into your spine.

4. As you exhale, rock back up to the starting position. Try to control the movement with your core muscles so that your feet do not touch the floor when you rock back up. If you have any trouble doing so, don't worry. This kind of balance takes quite a bit of practice to build.

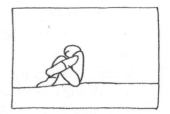

5. Repeat this rocking exercise five times, focusing on your breath and the sense of present awareness throughout the exercise.

## Practice 2: The Double Leg Stretch

1. Lie flat on the mat or floor with your arms resting at your sides and palms on the floor. Breathe deeply for five breaths, feeling the sensations of your body resting on the floor or mat.

2. Bring your attention to your core, your belly button, and concentrate on tensing your abdominal muscles. Focus on making your core feel solid and stable. Imagine your belly button rooted down into your spine. Throughout this flow, you will concentrate your attention on your core in this way.

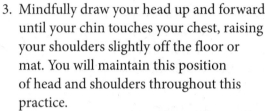

3. Mindfully draw your head up and forward until your chin touches your chest, raising your shoulders slightly off the floor or mat. You will maintain this position of head and shoulders throughout this practice.

4. As you inhale, bend your legs and draw your knees up toward your nose as far as you can. Place your hands on your shins below your knee in order to maintain stability in this part of the practice.

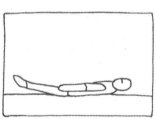

5. As you exhale, stretch your legs and arms back to their full length.

6. Complete five repetitions with both legs. Don't forget to coordinate the movement of your legs with the inhalation and exhalation of your breath.

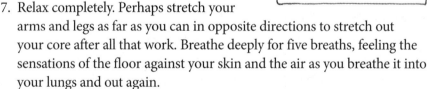

7. Relax completely. Perhaps stretch your arms and legs as far as you can in opposite directions to stretch out your core after all that work. Breathe deeply for five breaths, feeling the sensations of the floor against your skin and the air as you breathe it into your lungs and out again.

## Practice 3: The Swan Dive

1. Lie flat on the mat or floor with your face down. Keep your arms beside your body with your palms up toward the ceiling.

2. Take a moment to inhale and exhale, feeling the sensations of your body against the floor. Be present in this moment, and retain this focus for your awareness throughout the remainder of the exercise.

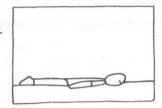

3. On your next inhalation, raise your head up and back and arch your back. Raise your arms up from the floor in a sideways line with your shoulders, forming a "T" shape.

4. Then raise your legs together off the floor as far as you can. In this way, you will curve off the floor, with only the torso area remaining in direct contact with the mat.

5. Keep your core, both abdominals and back, tensed throughout this movement.

6. As you exhale, gently rock forward so that the front of your body comes to the ground as your legs and feet rock higher off the ground. Then rock your legs and feet to the ground as your upper body and torso come off the ground.

7. Repeat this rocking exercise five times. Direct your mindful awareness to maintaining the proper form of the exercise throughout each repetition.

## Practice 4: The One Leg Kick

1. Lie facedown on the mat or floor with your head resting on your hands. Breathe deeply for five breaths, feeling the sensations of your body resting on the floor or mat.

2. Bring your attention to your core, your belly button, and concentrate on tensing your abdominal muscles. Focus on making your core feel solid and stable. Imagine your belly button rooted down into your

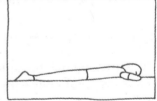

spine. Throughout this flow, you will concentrate your attention on your core in this way.

3. Slowly breathe in and begin to raise your upper body. Keep your pelvis, lower body, and legs pressed against the floor.

4. Continue raising up until your elbows are resting on the mat. Engage your abdominal muscles to lift your core up and in throughout the entirety of this practice.

5. On your next inhale, raise your right leg about two inches off the floor and kick it toward your buttocks.

6. Lower your right leg as you exhale. Then repeat this movement with your left leg.

7. Repeat this exercise five times for each leg. Bring your awareness to the sensations of your lower legs and feet. Notice any difficulty in feeling and controlling the movements when you cannot visually track what you are doing.

## Practice 5: The Neck Pull

1. Lie flat on the mat or floor with your arms behind your head and fingers interlaced. Breathe deeply for five breaths, feeling the sensations of your body resting on the floor or mat.

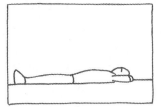

2. Bring your attention to your core, your belly button, and concentrate on tensing your abdominal muscles. Focus on making your core feel solid and stable. Imagine your belly button rooted down into your spine. Throughout this flow, you will concentrate your attention on your core in this way.

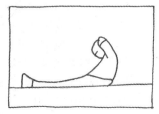

3. Draw your head to your chin, and slowly raise your body up and forward until you are in a seated position. Control of breath and movement are very important to this exercise. Do not sit up quickly and forcefully. Contrary to the name of the exercise, do not put pressure on your neck by pulling yourself up with your hands. Pull yourself up with your abdominal muscles alone.

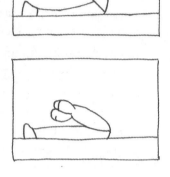

4. Bend your head forward and curve your spine so that you form a "C" shape as you stretch your head in the direction of your toes. Keep your fingers interlaced behind your head.

5. Then come up to a straight back position. Inhale deeply and begin to lower yourself while keeping a straight back as far as you are able to maintain control.

6. Finally, bend your head forward as you resume a lying down flat position on the mat.

7. Repeat this exercise three times. Do not use momentum between repetitions. Lie flat completely between sitting up each time.

## Practice 6: The Shoulder Bridge

1. Lie flat on the mat. Bend your knees and place your feet flat on the floor approximately hip width apart. Take a few moments to inhale and exhale. Bring the awareness of your mind to the sensations of your body. Feel the floor on which you are resting.

2. Bring your attention to your core, your belly button, and concentrate on tensing your abdominal muscles. Focus on making your core feel solid and stable. Imagine your belly button rooted down into your spine. Throughout this flow, you will concentrate your attention on your core in this way.

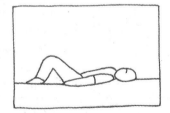

3. As you inhale, slowly raise your body up until you are resting on your upper arms, elbows, neck, shoulders, and head. Keep your feet flat on the floor with your buttocks pressed up as far as possible. Place your hands firmly on either side of your waist.

4. Straighten your right leg in front of you and raise it to a perpendicular position with the floor. Then lower it back to a parallel position with the floor. Repeat this up-and-down motion five times.

5. Lower down slowly to the mat. Curl down to the mat from the top of your spine until the bottom of your tailbone is resting on the mat. Do not simply drop down due to risk of spinal strain.

6. Repeat this series with your left leg.

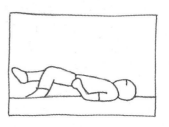

7. This complicated practice will need your full attention as you perform it. Be present with each movement as you make it. Breathe into it. Breathe out again. Never lose track of your breath.

## Practice 7: The Hip Twist

1. Begin this practice seated on your mat with your legs stretched out in front of you.

2. Stretch your arms behind you to brace yourself with palms pressed flat against the floor.

3. Bring your attention to your core, your belly button, and concentrate on tensing your abdominal muscles. Focus on making your core feel solid and stable. Imagine your belly button rooted down into your spine. Throughout this flow, you will concentrate your attention on your core in this way.

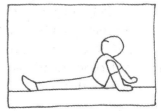

4. As you inhale, bring your legs up to about ten inches above the mat. Do not bend your knees or separate your legs. Keep your legs together throughout the entire exercise.

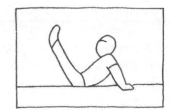

5. Take a few breaths here to focus your concentration before proceeding.

6. Slowly swing your legs so that your feet move in a clockwise direction. Move both your legs as far as you can to the right, and then swing them in a circular motion over to the left as far as possible.

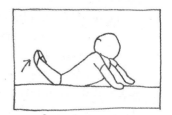

7. Complete this clockwise circle three times. Then perform the same motion in a counterclockwise manner for three more repetitions.

8. Be sure that only your legs and hips move throughout this exercise. Your upper body should remain immobile.

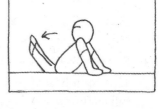

## Practice 8: The Swimming

1. Lie facedown on the mat or floor with your head resting on your hands. Breathe deeply for five breaths, feeling the sensations of your body resting on the floor or mat.

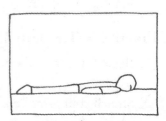

2. Bring your attention to your core, your belly button, and concentrate on tensing your abdominal muscles. Focus on making your core feel solid and stable. Imagine your belly button rooted down into your spine. Throughout this flow, you will concentrate your attention on your core in this way.

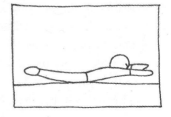

3. As you inhale, stretch your arms forward, keeping your palms facing down. Lift your head up and back off the mat or floor.

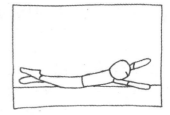

4. Raise your legs and toes of the ground, so that only your torso is resting on the ground.

5. As you inhale and exhale in a normal manner, move your arms and legs in opposition in the traditional motions for alternating overhand swimming strokes, or the "crawling" stroke.

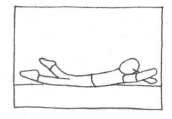

6. Perform these alternating strokes with arms and legs for a slow count of ten. Then lay down flat facedown and breathe in and out very deeply. Gather your focus.

7. Repeat another series of alternating strokes for a count of ten.

## Practice 9: The Leg Pull—Front

1. Come up to a traditional push-up position, beginning at the top of the movement with arms fully extended and elbows locked in place.

2. Bring your attention to your core, your belly button, and concentrate on tensing your abdominal muscles. Focus on making your core feel solid and stable. Imagine your belly button rooted down into your spine. Throughout this flow, you will concentrate your attention on your core in this way.

3. Raise your right leg off the mat and lift it as high as you can. Do not bend your knee; keep the leg straight. At your point of highest extension, feel the sensations of stretching in that leg and the weight of your body against the floor in the palms

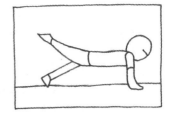

of your hands and the toes of your left leg. Take a deep inhale and exhale as you hold this point.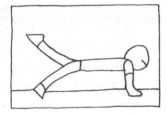

4. Lower your right leg back to the mat or floor.

5. Raise your left leg off the mat and lift it as high as you can. Do not bend your knee; keep the leg straight. At your point of highest extension, feel the sensations of stretching in that leg and the weight of your body against the floor in the palms of your hands and the toes of your right leg. Take a deep inhale and exhale as you hold this point.

6. Repeat the entire exercise five times. Breathe mindfully at the moment of pause when each leg is stretched up as high as you can hold.

## Practice 10: The Side Kick Kneeling

1. Kneel on your floor or mat, resting on your knees. Keep your upper body, pelvis, and thighs raised straight off the ground. Breathe deeply for five inhalations and exhalations at the beginning of this movement. Feel the sensations of your environment and the weight of your body on your knees.

2. Bring your attention to your core, your belly button, and concentrate on tensing your abdominal muscles. Focus on making your core feel solid and stable. Imagine your belly button rooted down into your spine. Throughout this flow, you will concentrate your attention on your core in this way.

3. Kneel on your left knee and place the palm of your left hand flat on the floor. Support the weight of your body on your left knee and left arm, and straighten your right leg out parallel from the floor.

4. Bend your right arm and place your right hand on the back of your head.

5. Keeping your right leg straight, swing your leg as far forward as possible without losing your balance. Breathe mindfully for one deep, slow inhalation and exhalation at this point.

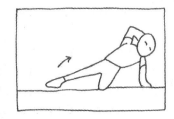

6. Next, swing your right leg as far back as possible without losing your balance. Breathe mindfully for one deep, slow inhalation and exhalation at this point.

7. Repeat these motions three times front and back with your right leg. Then slowly come back up to the position in step 1.

8. Repeat this series of movements balanced on your right knee and arm with your left leg swinging back and forth.

## Practice 11: The Rocking

1. Lie facedown on the mat or floor with your hands resting by your sides. Breathe deeply for five breaths, feeling the sensations of your body resting on the floor or mat.

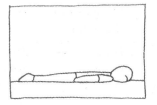

2. Bring your attention to your core, your belly button, and concentrate on tensing your abdominal muscles. Focus on making your core feel solid and stable. Imagine your belly button rooted down into your spine. Throughout this flow, you will concentrate your attention on your core in this way.

3. Bend your knees and bring your feet and lower legs up and forward. Simultaneously, reach your hands back to grab the tops of your feet. You will approximately form an oval position with your entire body.

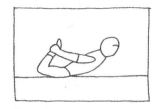

4. Take a deep full breath here. Feel the sensations of stretching throughout the length of

your body from the soles of your feet to the top of your head.

5. Gently begin to rock forward until your chin touches the mat or floor.

6. Use the momentum of your rocking to rock backward until your thighs touch the floor completely. This motion will draw your upper body off of the floor and into the air.

7. Continue this rocking stretch ten times. Try to perform a full circuit of rocking back and forth for each inhalation and another full circuit for each exhalation.

## HOW TO PRACTICE: ADVANCED SERIES

### Practice 1: The Roll Over

1. Lie flat on the mat or floor with your arms beside you with palms facing down. Breathe deeply for five breaths, feeling the sensations of your body resting on the floor or mat.

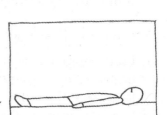

2. Bring your attention to your core, your belly button, and concentrate on tensing your abdominal muscles. Focus on making your core feel solid and stable. Imagine your belly button rooted down into your spine. Throughout this flow, you will concentrate your attention on your core in this way.

3. Slowly inhale and raise your legs up and over until your toes touch the mat or floor behind your head. If you are not flexible enough to actually touch the floor (I'm not), then stop at the point of greatest stretch without pain.

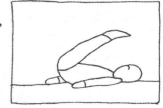

4. Spread your legs apart as far as possible. Breathe deeply in and out at this point. Pay

mindful attention to all the sensations of your body for the space of a deep inhalation and exhalation.

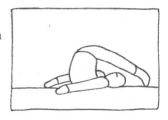

5. Slowly roll your spine back down to the ground until your legs are perpendicular to the floor. Then draw your legs back together.

6. Repeat this exercise five times.

7. Switch the motion. Begin with your legs spread as far apart as possible, roll up and over, then bring your legs back together at the top of the movement.

8. Slowly roll your spine back down to the ground until your legs are perpendicular to the floor. Then spread your legs wide once more.

9. Repeat this exercise five times.

## Practice 2: The Rocker with Open Legs

1. While sitting up on a mat, bend your knees and draw your legs to your chest. Bend forward to grab your ankles firmly. Do not cross your grip. Your right hand should be on your right ankle, and your left hand should be on your left ankle.

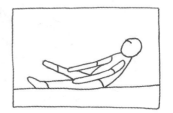

2. Bring your attention to your core, your belly button, and concentrate on tensing your abdominal muscles. Focus on making your core feel solid and stable. Imagine your belly button rooted down into your spine. Throughout this flow, you will concentrate your attention on your core in this way.

3. Slowly raise your legs up and straighten them out, locking your knees.

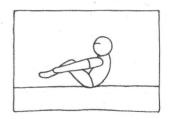

4. Breathe in deeply, mindfully, and concentrate on rocking yourself back by drawing your belly button further back into your spine.

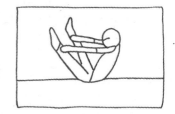

5. As you exhale, rock back up to the starting position. Try to control the movement with your core muscles so that you balance on your buttocks with your legs fully extending upward in the air. If you have any trouble doing so, don't worry. This kind of balance takes quite a bit of practice to build.

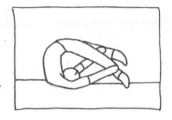

6. Repeat this rocking exercise five times, focusing on your breath and sense of present awareness throughout the exercise.

## Practice 3: The Cork Screw

1. Lie flat on the mat or floor with your arms beside you with palms facing down. Breathe deeply for five breaths, feeling the sensations of your body resting on the floor or mat.

2. Bring your attention to your core, your belly button, and concentrate on tensing your abdominal muscles. Focus on making your core feel solid and stable. Imagine your belly button rooted down into your spine. Throughout this flow, you will concentrate your attention on your core in this way.

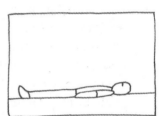

3. As you inhale, slowly raise your legs until your body rests on your shoulders, arms, and head. Take a moment to breathe deeply in and out once before proceeding. Balance the tension of this pose with a mindful awareness of this moment here and now.

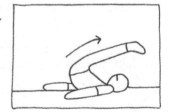

4. As you lower yourself down, twist your body to the right so that your toes are perpendicular to the floor and pause about two inches above the ground. Pause for one slow, deep breath.

5. Swing your legs back up to the middle and over, twisting toward the left in the same manner as the previous step. Pause with

your toes about two inches above the floor for a deep inhalation and exhalation.

6. Complete this entire circuit three times. Pause as needed to draw your focus back to a present awareness of the sensations of your body.

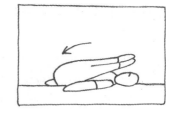

## Practice 4: The Jack Knife

1. Lie flat on the mat or floor with your arms beside you with palms facing down. Breathe deeply for five breaths, feeling the sensations of your body resting on the floor or mat.

2. Bring your attention to your core, your belly button, and concentrate on tensing your abdominal muscles. Focus on making your core feel solid and stable. Imagine your belly button rooted down into your spine. Throughout this flow, you will concentrate your attention on your core in this way.

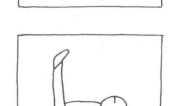

3. As you breathe in, lift your legs straight up until they are perpendicular to the floor. Do not bend your knees.

4. Continue raising yourself up until your spine is raised about five inches off the mat. Concentrate on engaging your abdominal muscles to maintain your balance and not roll over further. Take a deep, mindful breath at this point.

5. Lower yourself down to the position of step 3. Repeat steps 3 and 4 for five repetitions.

6. Do not forget to pause at the top of the movement, inhaling and exhaling a deep breath, mindfully controlling your balance and focusing on the sensations of your body in this present moment.

## Practice 5: The Teaser

1. Sit up straight on the mat or floor with your legs stretched out in front of you and with your arms resting at your sides with palms up. Breathe deeply for five breaths, feeling the sensations of your body resting on the floor or mat.

2. Bring your attention to your core, your belly button, and concentrate on tensing your abdominal muscles. Focus on making your core feel solid and stable. Imagine your belly button rooted down into your spine. Throughout this flow, you will concentrate your attention on your core in this way.

3. As you inhale, bring your chin to your chest, draw your abdominals in as you roll back to lay on the floor, keeping your head, neck, and shoulders off of the ground.

4. Raise your legs to forty-five degrees without bending your knees.

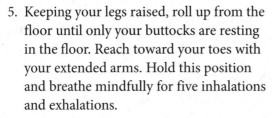

5. Keeping your legs raised, roll up from the floor until only your buttocks are resting in the floor. Reach toward your toes with your extended arms. Hold this position and breathe mindfully for five inhalations and exhalations.

6. Slowly lower back down so that your torso is resting on the floor. Take one more deep breath and bring your legs down to the floor and, last of all, your shoulders, neck, and head.

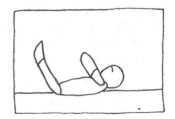

## Practice 6: The Leg Pull

1. Sit with your legs straight out in front of you. Keep your back straight.
2. Ground your hands firmly by your sides with palms down.

3. Push up your torso until your upper body, waist, and legs form one single line.

4. Stabilize your core by tensing your stomach and buttocks. Focus on not bending your waist throughout this exercise.

5. Raise your right leg up as high as you can. At the point of greatest extension, hold and breathe in and out deeply once. Then lower your leg back down.

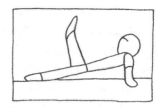

6. Raise your left leg up as high as you can. At the point of greatest extension, hold and breathe in and out deeply once. Then lower your leg back down.

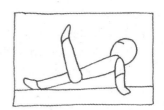

7. Repeat this entire exercise circuit five times.

8. Lower back down to a seated position with back straight. Take five more deep inhalations and exhalations. Close your eyes. Pay attention to the sensations that your body is registering through your other senses right now. Pause and take time in the middle of this challenging series to simply be.

## Practice 7: The Side Bend

1. From a seated position, shift to your right side. Take one deep breath here.

2. Bring your attention to your core, your belly button, and concentrate on tensing your abdominal muscles. Focus on making your core feel solid and stable. Imagine your belly button rooted down into your spine. Throughout this flow, you will concentrate your attention on your core in this way.

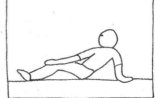

3. Ground yourself on your right hand, and push up until you form one straight line with your body, resting your weight on your outstretched right hand and the side of your right foot. Breathe deeply once here. Keep your abdominal muscles engaged to help you balance.

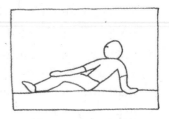

4. Lower your body until your right calf touches the mat or floor.

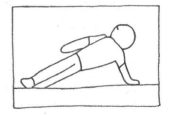

5. Press back up to the position you attained in step 3. Then sweep your left arm overhead to reach out in line with your body as far as you can.

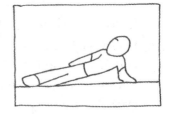

6. Repeat steps 3 to 5 for five repetitions. Then lower down to the position in step 1. Take a moment or two to breathe deeply here.

7. Shift over to the left side, and repeat these steps on your left.

## Practice 8: The Boomerang

1. Sit with your legs straight out in front of you. Keep your back straight.

2. Bring your attention to your core, your belly button, and concentrate on tensing your abdominal muscles. Focus on making your core feel solid and stable. Imagine your belly button rooted down into your spine. Throughout this flow, you will concentrate your attention on your core in this way.

3. Cross your left leg over your right leg.

4. Slowly inhale and raise your legs up and over until your toes touch the mat or floor behind your head. If you are not flexible enough to actually touch the floor (I'm

not), then stop at the point of greatest stretch without pain. Take a moment for one deep, mindful breath.

5. Rock back forward, but use your abdominal muscles to pause yourself before your legs touch the floor. Then, using your abdominal muscles, contract and draw your legs back up three inches toward your nose. After that slight contraction, go ahead and lower your legs to the floor.

6. Cross your right leg over your left leg and proceed through steps 4 thru 5 again.

7. Repeat this exercise five times, varying which leg is on top with each repetition. Focus your mindful attention at maintaining your balance and proceeding slowly through the circuit.

## Practice 9: The Seal

1. Sit with your knees bent and heels on the floor in front of you. Keep your back straight.

2. Bring your attention to your core, your belly button, and concentrate on tensing your abdominal muscles. Focus on making your core feel solid and stable. Imagine your belly button rooted down into your spine. Throughout this flow, you will concentrate your attention on your core in this way.

3. As you inhale, slowly bend your head toward your chest, and let your knees fall apart while you keep the soles of your feet together.

4. Intertwine your arms underneath your legs in order to grab your instep.

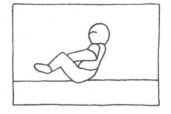

5. Click the soles of your feet together twice. Breathe in deeply, mindfully, and concentrate on rocking yourself back by drawing

your belly button further back into your spine. With your head resting on the mat, legs above you, and knees bent, click the soles of your feet twice again

6. As you exhale, rock back up to the starting position. Try to control the movement with your core muscles so that your feet do not touch the floor when you rock back up. If you have any trouble doing so, don't worry. This kind of balance takes quite a bit of practice to build.

7. Repeat steps 5 and 6 for five repetitions.

## Practice 10: The Crab

Sit with your legs straight out in front of you. Keep your back straight.

1. Bring your attention to your core, your belly button, and concentrate on tensing your abdominal muscles. Focus on making your core feel solid and stable. Imagine your belly button rooted down into your spine. Throughout this flow, you will concentrate your attention on your core in this way.

2. As you inhale slowly, cross your legs in traditional cross-legged position, and draw your head down toward your chest. Touch your chin to your chest if you are able.

3. Grasp your feet with opposite hands by intertwining your grip. Your left hand should grasp your right foot, and your right hand should grasp your left foot.

4. Breathe in deeply, mindfully, and concentrate on rocking yourself back by drawing your belly button further back into your spine.

5. Roll yourself back up and forward until your head touches the mat or floor in front of you. Then roll back once more. As you roll, switch which leg is on top.

6. Continue this rolling motion, punctuated by the switch in leg position for five repetitions. Synchronize your attention with your breathing. Breathe deeply and regularly as far as you are able for the duration of this circuit.

## Practice 11: The Control Balance

1. Lie flat on the mat or floor with your arms beside you with palms facing down. Breathe deeply for five breaths, feeling the sensations of your body resting on the floor or mat.

2. Bring your attention to your core, your belly button, and concentrate on tensing your abdominal muscles. Focus on making your core feel solid and stable. Imagine your belly button rooted down into your spine. Throughout this flow, you will concentrate your attention on your core in this way.

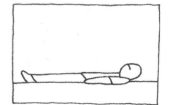

3. Slowly inhale and raise your legs up and over until your toes touch the mat or floor behind your head. If you are not flexible enough to actually touch the floor (I'm not), then stop at the point of greatest stretch without pain.

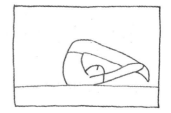

4. With your outstretched arms, grab hold of your ankles to stabilize your position. Your lower back should come off the floor, but keep your shoulders, neck, and head grounded throughout this entire exercise.

5. Keep your left leg and foot in this position, holding it with your left hand. As you inhale, let go of your right foot or ankle and raise your right leg up to a perpendicular position from the floor.

6. This exercise is the most difficult of all of Pilates' original exercises for one to maintain balance. Breathe mindfully into the balance of this hold. Remember to keep your abdominal muscles engaged. Let the sensations of your body guide you to the needed stillness to maintain here for a deep inhalation and exhalation.

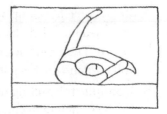

7. Then switch legs. Draw your right leg back down toward your head and the floor. Hold your right ankle or foot with your right hand while you raise your left leg up to a perpendicular position from the floor. Breathe mindfully here as well.

8. Repeat this entire circuit five times.

9. Slowly lower yourself back down to the position in step 1. As you lie flat on your back, take a few moments of rest. If your breathing is rapid, then take some time to allow it to return to your normal rate. As you breathe, focus on the sensations of your body. What are your five senses telling you right here, right now? Focus on taking this focused sense of presence with you in the rest of your day.

## VARIATIONS

Many variations are possible because there are so many variations on Pilates' original exercises. Please consult the "Resources for Further Study" on page 229 for several books that offer alternative exercises and flows. One of the simplest modifications is to perform all of Pilates' thirty-four exercises in their original order rather than in the three different series suggested above. There are also many wonderful video workouts for Pilates. I have noted my favorite series, but I do find that it is more difficult to maintain mindfulness when attempting to stay in step with a video. I like to consider myself as an "average" exerciser, and I often find that I have to exert quite a bit of "hustle" to keep up with the superbly athletic individuals who typically make workout videos.

# COMMON QUESTIONS

**Q:** What if I have trouble with the physical performance of a particular exercise?

**A:** I have chosen the exercises in the beginner series because they are the Pilates exercises that are typically easiest to perform without any special training. You might start there. With that said, if any particular exercise is too difficult to perform, please feel free to skip it or replace it in the flow with a different exercise from another Pilates routine. However, give yourself the space of going through one of the flows for five times or so before deciding to cut anything out. Everyone needs some time to get used to something new.

**Q:** What is the most essential part of the body flow series?

**A:** Almost everything from these body flows is adaptable, but there are two essential pieces. First, you must focus on your breathing and sensations mindfully. Second, the step of stabilizing your core is absolutely essential to Pilates. These two steps are the foundation on which you can build your own customized flow.

**Q:** Are these exercises inherently tied to a specific spiritual tradition?

**A:** Mindfulness practices originated within the religion of Buddhism. Pilates' methods were developed with a particular eye to Western (Greco-Roman) calisthenics, yoga, and ballet. However, both mindfulness and Pilates have been specifically divested of any overt religious content. As a result, the body flows suggested here are particularly applicable to any religious tradition. The body flows in chapter 25 deal with practices that have a closer connection to their religions of origin, but they are still potentially useful for someone from any religious or spiritual background.

**Q:** How should I breathe during the exercises?

**A:** Within Pilates proper, one is encouraged to breathe deeply in through the nose and exhale fully through the mouth. I find that this method is most effective for these flows as well.

**Q:** How long should I rest between exercises?

**A:** That amount of time is really up to you. You will likely want to rest at least thirty to sixty seconds between each exercise at first. Once you are familiar with each exercise in a series, you can begin to work on them as a single flow in which each exercise moves fluidly into the next.

Q: What if I have a mystical experience while performing the flow?

A: Mystical experiences are less common with practices that have a significant component of physical activity. However, if you do find yourself having a mystical experience of some sort, then you may want to stop the flow and sit in that moment for a while, perhaps even write down some insights or impressions. You may then wish to pick up the flow again. If you continue to exercise in the midst of such an intense experience, then you may risk injury due to the subsuming of your attention.

Q: Should these exercises be performed alone or in a group?

A: These body flows are particularly attuned to work as a group; perhaps they might even work best as part of a guided meditation or exercise class. However, I did develop these flows as individual activities, which is my particular bias when it comes to exercise of all sorts.

Q: What if I don't understand how to perform a certain exercise from your descriptive comments?

A: This is an entirely possible outcome. I did not understand how to perform several of Pilates' exercises just from his descriptions when I first started practicing this method. It may be quite helpful to go on a video streaming website, such as YouTube, and search for examples of a particular exercise being performed. I have retained all of Joseph Pilates' original names for the exercises included in this chapter, so you should be able to search successfully by combining the name of the exercise with Pilates' name.

Q: Could particular prayers be coupled with mindful breathing and Pilates' exercises?

A: It is possible, but I would not recommend lengthy prayers to be combined with these flows. The bulk of your concentration needs to be focused on your breathing and core stability, adding words to the mix is increasing the limit threshold for distraction.

Q: What if I simply cannot maintain mindful concentration during the flow?

A: Expect maintaining concentration to be difficult for the first several attempts. You will be building up mental muscles as well as physical ones here. However, if you simply cannot seem to build a satisfactory amount of focus during the flow after steady practice, then you may want to try out a different spiritual practice in its place. Alternatively, you may find that Pilates is an enriching physical exercise method, but you prefer to incorporate mindfulness into your life in different ways. Remember that the name of the game is experimentation. Never feel guilty for deciding that a particular practice is not the one for you.

## POTENTIAL JOURNALING PROMPTS OR DISCUSSION QUESTIONS

1. What positive experiences did you have while practicing this practice?
2. What negative experiences did you have while practicing this practice?
3. How did you adapt this structure to your situation?
4. What could be the benefits of learning to be present in your body through a flow of exercises?
5. Was it difficult to focus on how each part of your body felt in this practice? How? Why?

# 25

## Body Flow:
## Yoga with Centering Prayer

### BRIEF BACKGROUND

Here is one more series of body flow spiritual practices, a series of specific exercises or poses that a practitioner will move through in an unbroken sequence, moving directly from one to the next. As with any exercise routine, please consult with your primary care physician if you have any reservations about the level of exertion or any physical limitations that you may have. These particular flows, however, are meant to be gentler and more fluid than the ones presented in the last chapter. While Pilates' method focuses on increasing stability and strength, yoga puts relatively greater focus on flexibility and breath control.

Yoga has become well known in both the East and West, and it appears in both religious and nonreligious forms. As it first originated, the stretches associated with yoga were a small part of a much larger framework for living among spiritual seekers in Hinduism. The practitioners of yoga, often known by the term *yogi*, used certain stretches and poses with emphasis on the breath as the gateway to enlightenment. This viewpoint is not entirely alien to the Western mind since the word for breath and spirit originally had a very close relationship. If you are interested in the deeply religious forms of yoga in Hinduism, then you might consult some of the relevant works in the "Resources for Further Study" section on page 231. In this series, however, I will refer largely to a nonreligious view of yoga that concentrates on the stretches with comparatively less emphasis on the breathing aspect inherent in yoga.

As for centering prayer, you may want to revisit chapter 8 as a refresher of this practice. For the purposes of this series, I want to concentrate on using the sacred word from centering prayer as a means of focusing one's attention. Choose a word that is personally meaningful to you as a reminder to seek God within. In other words, you want a single word or short phrase to remind yourself of God whenever you realize that your mind has wandered off. Try not to change the word too often, especially during the body flow. You can use practically any word, including *God, love, hope, mercy,* or *mystery.* Ideally, as you go through the poses listed below, try to synchronize your breath and repetition of the word. However, this word is not a mantra. You are not attempting to repeat it endlessly or to the exclusion of awareness of your surroundings. Rather, repeat the sacred word as a way of redirecting your attention when you find that you have become distracted. For the purposes of demonstration, I will use the word *love* in the following steps, but feel free to use any word that resonates with you personally.

## HOW TO PRACTICE: BEGINNER SERIES

### Pose 1: Surrender

1. Stand up straight with feet apart and with hands by your sides, palms facing forward.
2. Raise your hands above your head and stretch as far as you can without your feet leaving the floor.
3. Stabilize your core by tensing your stomach. It may help to imagine "zipping" your belly button back to your spine.

4. Bending at your waist, while keeping your legs and back straight, reach your fingers to your toes. If you cannot reach your toes, reach as far as you can with feeling a stretch, not strain. Stretching to the point of pain is entirely counterproductive to the entire point of the body flow.
5. Maintain this position for twenty slow breaths. As you breathe, use the word *love* to draw your attention to the sensations of the pose and your connection to the spiritual.
6. Slowly raise yourself up until you are back in the position at step 1.

## Pose 2: Way of Christ

1. Stand up straight with feet together and with hands by your sides, palms facing forward.

2. Slowly raise your hands as far as you can above your head. Feel the stretch throughout your entire body, remembering to keep your feet rooted to the ground.

3. Cup your hands, with the palms facing each other and wrists touching one another.

4. In this position, with arms extended above and hands cupped, take ten slow, deep breaths.

5. Use the word *love* to center you in this pose of adoration for God, heaven, and/or the spiritual wonder of infinity.

6. Slowly lower your arms until you are back in the position at step 1.

## Pose 3: Steady Spirit

1. Stand up straight with feet together and with hands by your sides, palms facing forward.

2. Slowly bend at the waist with your arms and hands extended toward your toes. Feel a nice, easy stretch as you reach the point of slight resistance.

3. Bend your knees, and place your hands on the ground with palms flat.

4. "Walk" forward on your hands until your legs are straight. Your hips should be the highest point of an imaginary triangle, and your hands and feet should form the other angles. If you are familiar with traditional yoga poses, this is the "downward-facing dog" pose.

5. Take a few moments to inhale and exhale deeply in this pose. If you feel any tension in your body, then reflect on the word *love* to send love and relaxation to that tense spot.

6. Tread your feet in this position for a count of ten. Be very slow in your plodding along. Remember that slow and steady wins the race. If you find your attention wandering, then come back to the word *love* to focus your mind.

7. Bend your knees and walk your feet up to your hands. Straighten your knees to return to a traditional toe touch position.

8. Slowly raise yourself up until you are back in the position at step 1.

## Pose 4: Walking in the Way

1. Stand up straight with feet together and with hands by your sides, palms facing forward.

2. Shift your weight to your left foot.

3. Slowly raise your right foot and leg, as if you are going to take a very wide step.

4. Pause and hold for one slow, deep inhalation and exhalation as your leg is stretched in front of you with your knee slightly bent.

5. Bring your foot to the ground slowly.

6. Repeat on the other side.

7. Walk slowly in this manner for approximately five minutes. As you walk, return every so often to the word *love* and ponder how much we take for granted in the simple, often automatic, gift of walking.

## Pose 5: Receiving the Cosmic Christ

1. Stand up straight with feet together and with hands by your sides, palms facing forward.

2. Slowly raise your hands from your side until they are stretched out horizontally as far as you can reach. In this position, you will resemble the position of Christ on the cross at his crucifixion.

3. Breathe deeply, inhaling and exhaling, for ten repetitions with your arms extended

in this manner. Remember the word *love* here. Perhaps combine that word with the image of Christ on the cross to help center your attention.

4. Lower your hands back to your sides. Take one deep, full breath here, inviting an openness to love and Christ into your life, mind, spirit, and body.

5. Repeat this exercise three times.

## Pose 6: Yielding to the Spirit

1. Sit with your legs straight out in front of you. Keep your back straight.

2. Bend from your waist and reach your hands toward your shins.

3. Draw your head down toward your knees and your elbows toward the ground on either side of your legs. Reach down until you feel a stretch but no pain.

4. Hold this pose for ten slow, deep breaths. If your mind begins to wander, then remember *love*. Let this pose be a prayer of surrender to the work of the Spirit coming into your life.

5. Slowly raise yourself up until you return to the position in step 1.

## Pose 7: Enlivening the Spirit

1. Lie on the floor with your face toward the floor.

2. Slowly breathe in and begin to raise your upper body. Keep your pelvis, lower body, and legs pressed against the floor.

3. Continue raising up until your arms are straight and palms pressed flat against the floor. If you are familiar with traditional yoga postures, this is the "cobra" position.

4. Breathe deeply for ten repetitions. Feel each breath go up and down your spine. Remember the word *love*, and, perhaps, also remember

that the words for breath and spirit have a deep and ancient connection.

5. Bend your elbows and slowly lower your upper body back to the floor.

## Pose 8: Prayer

1. Sit in a kneeling position with your bottom resting on your heels while keeping your back straight.

2. Breathe in deeply, and, as you breathe out, bend forward from your waist, stretching your arms out in front of you and to the floor.

3. Keep reaching down until your palms, arms, and forehead touch the floor.

4. If you find that this stretch is too intense, slide your legs out from under your bottom, so that your bottom is resting on the floor rather than on your heels.

5. Slowly inhale and exhale as you rest in this pose. Relaxation is the intention of this pose, not stretching.

6. In synchronization with your breath, remember the word *love*. Make that single word the prayer of your heart.

7. Slowly raise yourself up to return to the position in step 1.

## Pose 9: Glory to God

1. Stand up straight with feet together and with hands by your sides, palms facing forward.

2. Shift the weight of your body to your right foot.

3. Slowly raise your left foot from the ground, bend your left knee, and place the foot against your right knee. If you are familiar with traditional yoga postures, this is the "tree" pose.

4. Bring your hands together with palms touching in front of your body.

5. If you have trouble keeping your balance, keep your eyes focused on a spot on the floor about three feet in front of you. If balance problems persist, you can rest one hand on a chair, bookshelf, or table until you can build the balance to rest on your right foot unassisted.

6. Slowly breathe in and out for five repetitions. Focus with the word *love* in this pose. Let love balance you.

7. Return to the position in step 1 and repeat with your other leg.

## Pose 10: Death and Resurrection

1. Lie flat on your back.

2. Let your arms spread out naturally with palms facing up.

3. Relax your legs by rotating your heels so that your toes point slightly out.

4. Feel yourself "sink" into the floor, and close your eyes.

5. Relax as deeply as possible, and breathe slowly, in and out, for ten repetitions.

6. As you relax and rest from this body flow, let your mind return to the word *love* and the meditation that love is the bridge between death and life.

7. You can continue this pose longer if you like, perhaps combining it with a more settled centering prayer time. Then get up and continue the "flow" of life.

# HOW TO PRACTICE: INTERMEDIATE SERIES

## Pose 1: Receptive

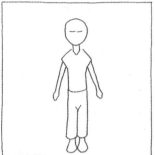

1. Stand up straight with feet together and with hands by your sides, palms facing forward.
2. Without moving your hands or feet, lengthen your body. Make your spine as tall as possible. Stretch your neck and head toward heaven. Root your legs and feet solidly into the earth.
3. Staying in this simple pose, relax and breathe deeply and slowly for five inhalations and exhalations.
4. As you breathe, bring the word *love* to the forefront of your mind. Let it rest lightly in your consciousness, focusing you on the present.

## Pose 2: Trinity

1. Stand up straight with feet together and with hands by your sides, palms facing forward.
2. With your next exhaled breath, step your left foot back as far as you can without bending your knee and point your toes out at a ninety-degree angle from your right foot.
3. Raise your arms to shoulder height, and reach your right arm out in front of you in line with your right foot. Reach your left arm behind you in the same line as your right arm. Do not align your left arm with your left foot.
4. Take one breath to settle into this pose.

5. Bend at your waist but keep your arms straight. Continue bending until you can touch your right shin or ankle with your right hand. Do not bend your knees.
6. Take five slow breaths in this "triangle" type pose. Then raise back up to the position of step 3. Breathe the word *love* to any point of tension in your legs or torso.
7. Repeat on the opposite side.

## Pose 3: Ascent

1. This pose will resemble pose 2 to a great extent. Stand up straight with feet together and with hands by your sides, palms facing forward.
2. With your next exhaled breath, step your left foot back as far as you can without bending your knee and point your toes out at a ninety-degree angle from your right foot.
3. Raise your arms to shoulder height, and reach your right arm out in front of you in line with your right foot. Reach your left arm behind you in the same line as your right arm. Do not align your left arm with your left foot.
4. Take one breath to settle into this pose.
5. Bend at your waist but keep your arms straight. Bend your right knee. Continue bending your torso until you can touch your right hand to the floor. Keep your left leg straight behind you.
6. Take five slow breaths as you stretch deeply with your right arm up in line with your head. Then raise back up to the position of step 3. Breathe the word *love* to any point of tension in your legs or torso.
7. Repeat on the opposite side.

## Pose 4: Peace with God

1. Stand up straight with feet together and with hands by your sides, palms facing forward.
2. With your next exhaled breath, step your left foot back as far as you can without bending your knee and point your toes out at a ninety-degree angle from your right foot.
3. Bend your right knee, but keep your left leg straight.
4. Raise your arms straight up above you and touch your palms together. Look up at your palms as you reach up.

5. Settle into this pose for five deep breaths. Use your sacred word as an expression of prayer as this pose orients you vertically in peaceful prayer to God above.

6. Return to the position of step 1 and repeat on the opposite side.

## Pose 5: Peace with Others

1. Stand up straight with feet together and with hands by your sides, palms facing forward.

2. With your next exhaled breath, step your left foot back as far as you can without bending your knee and point your toes out at a ninety-degree angle from your right foot.

3. Bend your right knee, but keep your left leg straight.

4. Raise your arms to shoulder height, and reach your right arm out in front of you in line with your right foot. Reach your left arm behind you in the same line as your right arm. Do not align your left arm with your left foot.

5. Settle into this pose for five deep breaths. Use love as an expression of community as this pose orients you horizontally in connection to all of humanity.

6. Return to the position of step 1 and repeat on the opposite side.

## Pose 6: Balanced Peace

1. Stand up straight with feet together and with hands by your sides, palms facing forward.

2. Ground yourself firmly on you left foot. Then begin to raise your right foot off the floor, moving behind you. Keep your knee straight.

3. Start to bend your upper body forward until you are making a "T" shape with your arms and right leg stretched in opposite directions. Your left leg remains

rooted firmly to the floor. You may need a chair to hold at first in order keep your balance.

4. Settle into this pose for five deep breaths. Use your sacred word as an expression of acceptance as this pose orients you internally to love yourself.

5. Return to the position of step 1 and repeat on the opposite side.

## Pose 7: Hope for the Future

1. Stand up straight with feet together and with hands by your sides, palms facing forward.

2. Stabilize your core by tensing your stomach. It may help to imagine "zipping" your belly button back to your spine.

3. Bending at your waist, while keeping your legs and back straight, reach your fingers to your shins. Look forward as you reach and concentrate on the straight line of your back.

4. Breathe deeply here, in and out, for five repetitions. Use the word *love* as a prayer for the unknown future ahead of you today. Let your pose remind you that you will look toward that future while remaining firmly grounded, yet always flexible.

5. Slowly rise back up to the position of step 1.

## Pose 8: Release the Past

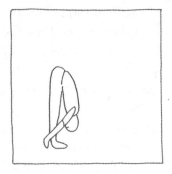

1. Stand up straight with feet together and with hands by your sides, palms facing forward.

2. Stabilize your core by tensing your stomach. It may help to imagine "zipping" your belly button back to your spine.

3. Bending at your waist, while keeping your legs and back straight, reach your fingers to your toes, then interlace your fingers behind your legs for a very deep stretch.

4. Breathe deeply here, in and out, for five repetitions. Use the word *love* as a prayer to let go of past mistakes. This pose, which is so close to the last one, will orient you toward an acceptance of what has gone before as finished. Today is a new day; release the past.

5. Slowly rise back up to the position of step 1.

## Pose 9: Yielding to the Spirit

1. Sit with your legs straight out in front of you. Keep your back straight.

2. Bend from your waist and reach your hands toward your shins.

3. Draw your head down toward your knees and your elbows toward the ground on either side of your legs. Reach down until you feel a stretch but no pain.

4. Hold this pose for five slow, deep breaths. If your mind begins to wander, then remember *love*. Let this pose be a prayer of surrender to the work of the Spirit coming into your life.

5. Slowly raise yourself up until you return to the position in step 1.

## Pose 10: Born Again

1. Sit with your legs straight out in front of you. Keep your back straight.

2. Ground your hands firmly by your sides with palms down.

3. Push up your torso until your upper body, waist, and legs form one single line.

4. Stabilize your core by tensing your stomach and buttocks. Focus on not bending your waist throughout this pose.

5. Hold here for five breaths. Use the word *love* to express the new energy and tension you feel in holding this pose. Imagine yourself being drawn upward while still being rooted to the floor by your hands and feet.

6. Slowly lower yourself down until you are back in the position at step 1.

## Pose 11: Turn to Christ

1. Sit with your legs straight out in front of you. Keep your back straight.

2. Begin to twist in your right side, placing your right palm on the floor behind you. Look over your right shoulder behind you. Do not move your hips or legs.

3. As you feel a stretch in your spine and upper body, concentrate on how your life is being stretched toward Christ. While it may not always be comfortable, you are being opened up to a new range of life. Use the word *love* to enter into this spiritual space.

4. Take five deep breaths as you relax into this position.

5. Slowly return to the position in step 1. Then repeat on the opposite side.

## Pose 12: Here Am I

1. Sit in a kneeling position with your bottom resting on your heels while keeping your back straight.

2. Stretch your head up as far as you can, lengthening out your head and neck.

3. Rest your hands on your knees with elbows straight.

4. Sit here and breathe for five deep breaths, or even ten deep breaths, if you find yourself fatigued. This pose is very gentle and restorative.

5. As you breathe, let the word *love* flow over you and take it into your inner self as self-acceptance.

6. Slowly return to the position in step 1.

## Pose 13: Send Me

1. Sit in a kneeling position with your bottom resting on your heels while keeping your back straight.

2. Rise up from this position until you are resting on your knees, shins, and the front of your feet.

3. Carefully lift your head and neck up and back, and stretch your upper body behind you.

4. As the stretch intensifies, reach your arms and hands behind you, resting your hands on your ankles behind you. If that stretch is too intense for your lower back (which is true for me), then reach your arms up above and back behind your head as seen in the second picture.

4. At the point of the stretch that best suits you, hold and breathe for five deep breaths. Use the word *love* to focus you on your present experience. Be right here, right now.

5. Slowly uncurl your spine. Then lower yourself back to the position in step 1.

## Position 14: Loyal Commitment

1. Stand up straight with feet together and with hands by your sides, palms facing forward.

2. Slowly bend at the waist with your arms and hands extended toward your toes. Feel a nice, easy stretch as you reach the point of slight resistance.

3. Bend your knees, and place your hands on the ground with palms flat.

4. "Walk" forward on your hands until your legs are straight. Your hips should be the highest point of an imaginary triangle, and your hands and feet should form the other angles. If you are familiar with traditional yoga poses, this is the "downward-facing dog" pose.

5. Take five deep breaths to inhale and exhale in this pose. If you feel any tension in your body, then reflect on the word *love* to send love and relaxation to that tense spot.

6. Continue meditating on your own commitment to spirituality and the reality behind all of our spiritual practices.

7. Then bend your knees and walk your feet back toward your hands.

8. Once you are back in a toe touch position, give yourself one more moment to stretch here, and stand back up to resume the position in step 1.

## Position 15: World Upside Down

1. Lie flat on your back.

2. Take a moment to tense your stomach and torso. Keep these muscles engaged throughout this pose.

3. Slowly lift your legs up, keeping the legs together.

4. Continue lifting until your lower body comes off the floor. Then place both hands on the small of your back for stability.

5. You should find yourself in a traditional "shoulder stand" position. Your head, shoulders, upper arms, and elbows should remain on the floor throughout this pose.

6. Take five deep breaths here. Stabilize, balance, and focus yourself at the end of this series with your sacred word *love*. As you are physically experiencing inversion, consider how the love of Christ turns your world upside down, or, perhaps, it is love which turns each of our worlds right side up.

7. Slowly lower yourself back to the floor, and lie flat on your back for a few moments to pause before going on with your day. Remember your word of intention: *love*. Take love with you throughout the remainder of your day.

# HOW TO PRACTICE: ADVANCED SERIES

This final series incorporates several of the poses presented in the beginner and intermediate series with the addition of a few challenging poses. The major difference, however, is that the advanced poses are truly meant to flow one into the other. So while you will pause for some deep breathing in each pose, please proceed directly from one pose into the next one. It may be difficult to establish a true flow for the first few sessions, but once you are familiar with the poses and their order, then the flow will come much more naturally and easily.

## Flow 1: Meditation

In these flows, it is vitally important to consult the accompanying illustrations to make sense fully of each instructional step.

1.  Stand up straight with feet together and with hands by your sides, palms facing forward. Take five breaths here. Breathe in and out your sacred word.
2.  Slowly raise your hands as far as you can above your head. Feel the stretch throughout your entire body, remembering to keep your feet rooted to the ground.
3.  Raise your arms straight up above you and touch your palms together. Look up at your palms as you reach up. Take five breaths here. Meditate on your word *love*.
4.  Bending at your waist, while keeping your legs and back straight, reach your fingers to your toes. Take five breaths here. Continue concentrating on love and its many facets.
5.  Come up slightly, while keeping your legs and back straight, reach your fingers to your shins. Look forward as you reach and concentrate on the straight line of your back. Take five breaths in order to pause here.
6.  Lower yourself into a traditional push-up position. Then lower yourself until your arms are bent at a ninety-degree angle. Hold in this half push-up pose for another five deep breaths. It is likely that this step will be quite difficult at first. Breathe into the tension you feel. Send thoughts of love where you feel difficulty in your body.

7. Slowly breathe in and begin to raise your upper body. Keep your pelvis, lower body, and legs pressed against the floor. Continue raising up until your arms are straight and palms pressed flat against the floor. Take five breaths at this point in the flow. Meditate on your word *love*, sending that love out toward your family, friends, and all of humanity.

8. Begin to bend your waist to press up, and "walk" forward on your hands until your legs are straight. Your hips should be the highest point of an imaginary triangle, and your hands and feet should form the other angles. Take five breaths here, using your prayer word to express your commitment to God and your own process of spiritual seeking.

9. Come up slightly, returning to the position from step 5. While keeping your legs and back straight, reach your fingers to your shins. Look forward as you reach and concentrate on the straight line of your back. Take five breaths in order to pause here.

10. Then return to the position from step 4. While keeping your legs and back straight, reach your fingers to your toes. Take five breaths here. Continue concentrating on love and its many facets.

11. Rise up to resume the position from step 3. Raise your arms straight up above you and touch your palms together. Look up at your palms as you reach up. Take five breaths here. Meditate on your word *love*.

12. End this flow where you began in step 1. Stand up straight with feet together and with hands by your sides, palms facing forward. Take five breaths here. Breathe in and out your sacred word.

## Flow 2: Contemplation

Even as meditation and contemplation are connected and yet separate in the Christian tradition, flow 1 and flow 2 of this series are closely related. Contemplation goes further than meditation, and you might think (as I did the first time I tried it) that this flow requires divine assistance. In other words, this flow is quite physically challenging.

1. Stand up straight with feet together and with hands by your sides, palms facing forward. Take five breaths here. Breathe in and out your sacred word.

2. Slowly raise your hands as far as you can above your head. Feel the stretch throughout your entire body, remembering to keep your feet rooted to the ground.

3. Raise your arms straight up above you and touch your palms together. Look up at your palms as you reach up. As you do so, bend your knees, as if you are sitting in a chair. Hold this "sitting" pose for five breaths. Breathe your word *love* into any tension you begin to feel in your legs.

4. Bending at your waist, while keeping your legs and back straight, reach your fingers to your toes. Take five breaths here. Continue concentrating on love and its many facets.

5. Come up slightly, while keeping your legs and back straight, reach your fingers to your shins. Look forward as you reach and concentrate on the straight line of your back. Take five breaths in order to pause here.

6. Lower yourself into a traditional push-up position. Then lower yourself until your arms are bent at a ninety-degree angle. Hold in this half push-up pose for another five deep breaths. It is likely that this step will be quite difficult at first. Breathe into the tension you feel. Send thoughts of love where you feel difficulty in your body.

7. Slowly breathe in and begin to raise your upper body. Keep your pelvis, lower body, and legs pressed against the floor. Continue raising up until your arms are straight and palms pressed flat against the floor. Take five breaths at this point in the flow. Meditate on your word *love*, sending that love out toward your family, friends, and all of humanity.

8. Begin to bend your waist to press up, and "walk" forward on your hands until your legs are straight. Your hips should be the highest point of an imaginary triangle, and your hands and feet should form the other

angles. Take five breaths here, using your prayer word to express your commitment to God and your own process of spiritual seeking.

9. With your next exhaled breath, step your left foot back as far as you can without bending your knee and point your toes out at a ninety-degree angle from your right foot. Bend your right knee, but keep your left leg straight. Raise your arms straight up above you and touch your palms together. Look up at your palms as you reach up. Settle into this pose for five deep breaths. Use your sacred word as an expression of prayer as this pose orients you vertically in peaceful prayer to God above.

10. Lower yourself into a traditional push-up position. Then lower yourself until your arms are bent at a ninety-degree angle. Hold in this half push-up pose for another five deep breaths. It is likely that this step will be quite difficult at first. Breathe into the tension you feel. Send thoughts of love where you feel difficulty in your body.

11. Slowly breathe in and begin to raise your upper body. Keep your pelvis, lower body, and legs pressed against the floor. Continue raising up until your arms are straight and palms pressed flat against the floor. Take five breaths at this point in the flow. Meditate on your word *love*, sending that love out toward your family, friends, and all of humanity.

12. Begin to bend your waist to press up, and "walk" forward on your hands until your legs are straight. Your hips should be the highest point of an imaginary triangle, and your hands and feet should form the other angles. Take five breaths here, using your prayer word to express your commitment to God and your own process of spiritual seeking.

13. With your next exhaled breath, step your right foot back as far as you can without bending your knee and point your toes out at a ninety-degree angle from your left foot. Bend your left knee, but keep your right leg straight. Raise your arms straight up above you and touch your palms together. Look up at your palms as you reach up. Settle into this pose for five deep breaths. Use your sacred word as an expression of prayer as this pose orients you vertically in peaceful prayer to God above.

14. Lower yourself into a traditional push-up position. Then lower yourself until your arms are bent at a ninety-degree angle. Hold in this half push-up pose for another five deep breaths. It is likely that this step will be quite difficult at first. Breathe into the tension you feel. Send thoughts of love where you feel difficulty in your body.

15. Slowly breathe in and begin to raise your upper body. Keep your pelvis, lower body, and legs pressed against the floor. Continue raising up until your arms are straight and palms pressed flat against the floor. Take five breaths at this point in the flow. Meditate on your word *love*, sending that love out toward your family, friends, and all of humanity.

16. Begin to bend your waist to press up, and "walk" forward on your hands until your legs are straight. Your hips should be the highest point of an imaginary triangle, and your hands and feet should form the other angles. Take five breaths here, using your prayer word to express your commitment to God and your own process of spiritual seeking.

17. Come up slightly, while keeping your legs and back straight, reach your fingers to your shins. Look forward as you reach and concentrate on the straight line of your back. Take five breaths in order to pause here.

18. While keeping your legs and back straight, reach your fingers to your toes. Take five breaths here. Continue concentrating on love and its many facets.

19. Come back up to a standing position. Raise your arms straight up above you and touch your palms together. Look up at your palms as you reach up. As you do so, bend your knees, as if you are sitting in a chair. Hold this "sitting" pose for five breaths. Breathe your word *love* into any tension you begin to feel in your legs.

20. Stand up straight with feet together and with hands by your sides, palms facing forward. Take five breaths here. Breathe in and out your sacred word.

## Flow 3: Perseverance

One of the most important aspects of the spiritual quest and all forms of love is perseverance, which is that ability to stick to our commitments even when our enthusiasm or physical energy is low. Let this combined flow of Release the Past, Trinity, and Ascent remind you of perseverance on the mystical path.

1. Stand up straight with feet together and with hands by your sides, palms facing forward.

2. Stabilize your core by tensing your stomach. It may help to imagine "zipping" your belly button back to your spine.

3. Bending at your waist, while keeping your legs and back straight, reach your fingers to your toes, then interlace your fingers behind your legs for a very deep stretch.

4. Breathe deeply here for five inhalations and exhalations. Rest in love.

5. With your next exhaled breath, step your left foot back as far as you can without bending your knee and point your toes out at a ninety-degree angle from your right foot.

6. Raise your arms to shoulder height, and reach your right arm out in front of you in line with your right foot. Reach your left arm behind you in the same line as your right arm. Do not align your left arm with your left foot.

7. Take one breath to settle into this pose.

8. Bend at your waist but keep your arms straight. Continue bending until you can touch your right shin or ankle with your right hand. Do not bend your knees.

9. Take five slow breaths in this "triangle" type pose. Then raise back up to the position of step 6. Breathe the word *love* to any point of tension in your legs or torso.

10. Repeat on the opposite side.

11. With your next exhaled breath, step your left foot back as far as you can without bending your knee and point your toes out at a ninety-degree angle from your right foot.

12. Raise your arms to shoulder height, and reach your right arm out in front of you in line with your right foot. Reach your left arm behind you in the same line as your right arm. Do not align your left arm with your left foot.

13. Take one breath to settle into this pose.

14. Bend at your waist but keep your arms straight. Bend your right knee. Continue bending your torso until you can touch your right hand to the floor. Keep your left leg straight behind you.

15. Take five slow breaths as you stretch deeply with your right arm up in line with your head. Then raise back up to the position of step 12. Breathe the word *love* to any point of tension in your legs or torso.

16. Repeat on the opposite side.

## Flow 4: Ground of the Soul

This flow is a bit less intense than the previous ones, so relax a bit here in order to re-center yourself. Connect through the word *love* to the ground of your soul, the center of your spirit, the image or "spark" of divinity at the core of your being.

1. Stand up straight with feet as wide apart as possible without bending your knees and with hands by your sides, palms facing forward.

2. Begin to bend at the waist, and continue to bend until the palms of your hands are flat on the ground and, perhaps, your head too, if flexibility allows.

3. Take five deep breaths at this point. Center yourself in the word *love* and the human depths, which it represents.

4. Lift up slightly, so that you can put your hands on your hips while still leaning forward. You may feel like you will fall forward. If so, just concentrate on grounding your feet firmly in order to maintain your balance.

5. Take five deep breaths here. Return to your word of meditation again, as you breathe.

6. Now interlace your fingers behind your back, and rotate your arms over your head as far as you can. Once again, ground your feet firmly in the same wide stance in order to keep from tipping over.

7. Take five deep breaths here. Let the word *love* help you to release the tension in your neck, shoulders, and upper back.

8. Finally, reach your hands toward your feet. Touch the toes of your right foot with your right hand. Touch the toes of your left foot with your left hand. Keep both arms and legs straight out at full extension.

9. Take five deep breaths here. Let the word *love* flow into the stretch you feel in the back of your legs and in your arms.

10. Slowly rise up to stand. Then bring your legs closer to each other until you resume a normal standing position. Take one more deep breath here to end the flow.

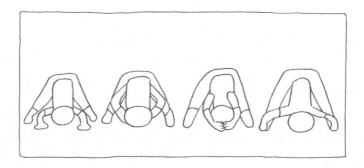

## Flow 5: Faith

This is a particularly challenging flow. You will test your balance, and it is perfectly acceptable to balance yourself by setting a hand on a chair as you first start out. As you breathe the word *love* in and out during this flow, concentrate on the interrelationship and necessity of both love and faith in the spiritual journey.

1. Stand up straight with feet together and with hands by your sides, palms facing forward.

2. Draw your hands back up behind you. If possible, place palms together with fingers pointing up to heaven. If this position is too difficult, just hold on to opposite elbows.

3. With your next exhaled breath, step your left foot back as far as you can without bending your knee and point your toes out at a ninety-degree angle from your right foot.

4. Keeping your arms and hands as in step 2, bend forward at the waist so that the top of your head comes down toward your foot, and your nose will draw toward your knee. If you are more flexible than I am, you might even be able to touch your nose to your knee.

5. Take five deep breaths at this point. Let your word of love move in and out of your spirit as the air moves in and out of your lungs.

6. Repeat on the opposite side.

7. Resume the position in step 1.

8. Slowly raise up your right leg with knee straight until it is parallel with the floor. Then reach out with your right arm, and hook the first two fingers of your right hand around your right toe to balance in this difficult standing position. Take five deep breaths. Maintain your balance physically as you meditate on how love helps you maintain the balance of your faith.

9. While in this same position, slowly swing your leg out to the right and turn your head to the left. These motions will intensify the stretch. Remember the word *love* to help you balance as you take five more deep breaths.

10. Bring your leg back to the center. Look forward once more. Then draw your leg up toward your nose, keeping the knee straight. Conversely, it might be more helpful to bend your upper body down toward your leg in order to maintain balance. Take five deep breaths here. Think of love and faith. Hold on to this pose.

11. Now let go of your leg, and take five more breaths as you hold your leg out parallel to the floor. Place your hands on your hips.

12. Repeat steps 7–11 on the opposite side.

# Flow 6: Sent

As the final flow in this difficult series, remember that the purpose of spiritual practice is not to simply store up good feelings and experiences for your own enjoyment. Spiritual practice thrusts us back into the world to bring our newly changed, or reinvigorated, attitude to the people and tasks around us. The spiritual journey always leads us back to the seemingly mundane, but truly beautiful, "normal" life. Let this flow lead you back.

1. Stand up straight with feet together and with hands by your sides, palms facing forward.

2. Shift the weight of your body to your right foot.

3. Slowly raise your left foot from the ground, bend your left knee, and place the foot against your right knee. If you are familiar with traditional yoga postures, this is the "tree" pose.

4. Bring your hands together with palms touching in front of your body.

5. If you have trouble keeping your balance, keep your eyes focused on a spot on the floor about three feet in front of you. If balance problems persist, you can rest one hand on a chair, bookshelf, or table until you can build the balance to rest on your right foot unassisted.

6. Slowly breathe in and out for five repetitions. Focus with the word *love* in this pose. Let *love* balance you.

7. Return to the position in step 1 and repeat with your other leg.

8. Come back up to a standing position. Raise your arms straight up above you and touch your palms together. Look up at your palms as you reach up. As you do so, bend your knees, as if you are sitting in a chair. Hold this "sitting" pose for five breaths. Breathe your word *love* into any tension you begin to feel in your legs.

9. With your next exhaled breath, step your left foot back as far as you can without bending your knee and point your toes out at a ninety-degree angle from your right foot. Bend your right knee, but keep your left leg straight. Raise your arms straight up above you and touch your palms together. Look up at your palms as you reach up. Settle into this pose for five deep breaths. Use your sacred word as an expression of prayer as this pose orients you vertically in peaceful prayer to God above.

10. Repeat step 9 on the opposite side.

11. With your next exhaled breath, step your left foot back as far as you can without bending your knee and point your toes out at a ninety-degree angle from your right foot. Bend your right knee, but keep your left leg straight. Raise your arms to shoulder height, and reach your right arm out in front of you in line with your right foot. Reach your left arm behind you in the same line as your right arm. Do not align your left arm with your left foot. Settle into this pose for five deep breaths. Use your sacred word as an expression of community as this pose orients you horizontally in connection to all of humanity.

12. Repeat step 11 on the opposite side.

## VARIATIONS

Many of the variations on centering prayer mentioned in chapter 8 also apply here, although they may need a little bit of adaptation. Additionally, there are multitudinous yoga poses and flows available in both religious and nonreligious venues. This initial series of practices is only meant as an introductory taste. Especially if you have practiced yoga previously, you may want to attempt more challenging poses. As with most other practices in this book, feel free to experiment and adapt to your individual needs and preferences. Do not feel limited to go through a body flow in exactly the same way every time because it gets easier for your mind to wander as your body becomes familiar with the poses.

## COMMON QUESTIONS

**Q:** Can I change the order of poses in the flows?

**A:** Absolutely. Mix and match the poses as you like. However, I recommend that you begin with a very gentle pose or two in order to warm up a bit as you stretch. Similarly, I recommend ending the beginner flow with the "Death and Resurrection" pose regardless of what poses you have utilized in the rest of the body flow. This pose is the most effective one for grounding you as you end the body flow. Additionally, as noted in the steps for this pose, it transitions easily to a time of centering prayer. There are few better ways to lead into centering prayer than with a series of physical movements that awaken your body and bring your attention to its sensations.

**Q:** Are centering prayer and yoga compatible?

**A:** Centering prayer did arise out of the Christian spiritual tradition, and yoga did arise out of the Hindu spiritual tradition. While there are pieces of both practices that are tied to that tradition and may not "translate" easily to a new context, there are many points of compatibility and intersection that are ripe for experimentation. As with most of the practices in this book, try out to see if they are compatible for you in the mosaic of your own spiritual practice. That's the true litmus test of the compatibility of spiritual practices: Do they work for real people in the real world?

**Q:** Is there an essential piece to this practice that always needs to be there?

**A:** Yes, there is one essential piece to these body flows, and it is the hinge that ties centering prayer and yoga together:breathing. Attention and focus on the breath is vital in these body flows. The poses may vary, the sacred word may change, but the rhythm of your breath is the constant nexus for this practice.

**Q:** Can these body flows be done in a group?

**A:** Yes, while these body flows are presented in the context of a single practitioner, it is easily adaptable to group work. Interestingly, these body flows are even more suited to a group setting than those in the previous chapter. There are many centering prayer groups, and there are many yoga classes. It should not be too much of a stretch (pun intended) to put the two together.

**Q:** What if I have physical trouble with a particular stretch or pose?

**A:** If you are experiencing any type of physical difficulty in this practice, please consult a health care professional. I have chosen these exercises because they are notably gentle, offering a lot of promise for building concentration and focus in the flow. However, if you are experiencing too much physical difficulty in this practice, back off from the intensity of the stretches or substitute other poses as needed. Please make these flows your own. Do not feel restricted by the suggestions that I have made.

**Q:** What if I have a mystical experience during the flow?

**A:** While yoga does have more history in inducing mystical experience than Pilates, these types of experiences are less common with practices that have a significant component of physical activity. However, if you do find yourself having a mystical experience of some sort, then you may want to stop the flow and sit in that moment for a while, perhaps even write down some insights or impressions. You may then wish to pick up the flow again. If you continue to exercise in the midst of such an intense experience, then you may risk injury due to inattention to your physical environment.

**Q:** Are there any particular benefits to using these flows instead of trying yoga or centering prayer separately?

**A:** Not particularly. Try them separately. Try them together. See what works for you. Still, if you find yourself dozing off a little too often in your centering prayer practice, then these body flows may offer a practical antidote to the problem.

**Q:** Could I combine yoga with lengthier prayers?

**A:** Yes, if you so desire, then give it a try. One of the resources recommended in the "Resources for Further Study" section connects yoga and the Jesus Prayer. You might also try combining yoga and the Lord's Prayer. If you want to really challenge your depth of focus, then you can couple yoga with the prayers of the Rosary. If you do so, then you might want to revisit chapter 16 for a refresher. Try meditation on one of the "Mysteries" as a short transition between poses.

## POTENTIAL JOURNALING PROMPTS
## OR DISCUSSION QUESTIONS

1. What positive experiences did you have while practicing this practice?
2. What negative experiences did you have while practicing this practice?
3. How did you adapt this structure to your situation?
4. What could be the benefits of learning to be present in your body through a flow of exercises?
5. Was it difficult to focus on how each part of your body felt in this practice? How? Why?

# Conclusion

Here we are. We're at the end. I hope that you have found some intriguing practices along the way. Have you experimented with them? Have you adapted them? Have you found a practice or several practices that click with you? Remember that this sourcebook is meant to show what practices are not a good fit as well as those that are. Return as many times as you like to different sections. As a last word, I would like to remind you of two essential pieces for spiritual practice.

## BEGINNING

First, I would like to return to Thomas Merton. In the introduction, I left you with this quote by Merton: "We do not want to be beginners. But let us be convinced of the fact that we will never be anything else but beginners all our life." While it might seem counterintuitive, remember to be a beginner. Let's begin, and begin, and begin . . . each and every day. We have now gone through several different types of practices arising from diverse sources. Finding out what practices and types of practices resonate with you personally has required at least a bit of soul searching. On the spiritual quest, how are you walking? Do you seek a spirituality of concentrating, interiorizing, and filling up your mind? If so, you likely found value in the Meditating section. Do you seek a spirituality of contemplating and quieting the restless waters of your mind in order to hear the voice of God? If so, you likely found value in the Listening section. Do you seek a spirituality of awareness to the present moment, of right here, right now? If so, you likely found value in the Being section. Do you seek a spirituality that engages the tactile dimensions of life? If so, you likely found value in the Sensing section. Do you seek a vigorous spirituality, intertwining the physical, mental, and spiritual? If so, you likely found value in the Embodying section.

It is my sincere hope and prayer that you found value in multiple sections, mixing and matching practices as they fit you best. After all, this spiritual journey is your own, and your greatest regret could be trying to walk someone else's path. Let the words of Thomas Merton speak to us once again on the need to walk our own way:

> Many poets are not poets for the same reason that many religious men are not saints: they never succeed in being themselves. They never get around to being the particular poet or the particular monk they are intended to be by God. They never become the man [or woman] or the artist who is called for by all the circumstances of their individual lives. They waste their years in vain efforts to be some other poet, some other saint. . . . They wear out their minds and bodies in a hopeless endeavor to have someone else's experiences or write somebody else's poems.[1]

So, if nothing else, walk your own path—the poetry of your own spirituality.

## DOING

As you create your own way, there is one more essential piece to remember. I have written a lot about how to begin certain practices, and I have offered variations along with the types of temperaments that might find each one useful. I have not, however, said much about the purpose of the spiritual life in general. This lack of goal-oriented structure is intentional on my part. Spirituality is intensely personal, and it's not a little quirky. Throughout history, mystics from various religions have had experiences, insights, and messages that did not fit the approved mold of their society or, often, the shape of institutional religion. With one eye looking back, I don't want to be too prescriptive of what should happen in spiritual practice; rather, I want to encourage you, and myself, to be open to the surprises waiting along the way. I would be remiss if I did not include one final comment about purpose. Whatever our own experiences may be, the spiritual quest is about giving us a new perspective. I believe this perspective is best exemplified in the famous prayer of St. Patrick, a version of which reads:

> Christ with me, Christ before me, Christ behind me,
> Christ in me, Christ beneath me, Christ above me,
> Christ on my right, Christ on my left,

---

1. Thomas Merton, *New Seeds of Contemplation* (New York: New Directions, 2007), 98.

Christ when I lie down, Christ when I sit down,

Christ in the heart of everyone who thinks of me,

Christ in the mouth of everyone who speaks to me,

Christ in the eye that sees me,

Christ in the ear that hears me.

The spiritual quest is about shifting our perspective. It's not esoteric, meta-physical, or obscure. It's allowing ourselves to see the wonder in everyday life. It's allowing ourselves to see the goodness shining from the core of every person, even if--especially if--they can't see that goodness in themselves. With that thought in mind, let us turn our other eye toward the future and end with this prayer by Pierre Teilhard de Chardin, one of my favorite theologians:

> Up to now human beings lived apart from each other, scattered around the world and closed in upon themselves. They have been like passengers who accidentally met in the hold of a ship, not even suspecting the ship's motion. Clustered together on the earth, they found nothing better to do than to fight or amuse themselves. Now, by chance, or better, as a natural result of organization, our eyes are beginning to open. The most daring among us have climbed to the bridge. They have seen the ship that carries us all. They have glimpsed the ship's prow cutting the waves. They have noticed that a boiler keeps the ship going and a rudder keeps it on course. And, most important of all, they have seen clouds floating above and caught the scent of distant islands on the horizon. It is no longer agitation down in the hold, just drifting along; the time has come to pilot the ship. It is inevitable that a different humanity must emerge from this vision.[2]

Now that we have begun, let's continue to do and see what visions the future may hold, what forms of humanity will emerge. Who will you become?

---

2. de Chardin, *Activation of Energy*, 73–74.

# Resources for Further Study

## Chapter 1: The Jesus Prayer

Anonymous. *Philokalia: The Eastern Christian Spiritual Texts*. Translated by G. E. H. Palmer, Philip Sherrard, and Kallistos Ware. Woodstock, VT: SkyLight Paths, 2006.

The *Philokalia* is the oldest and most central mystical text for Eastern Orthodoxy. Consult this work if you want to know the background context for the Jesus Prayer. Beware that this is not light reading.

Anonymous. *The Way of a Pilgrim* and *The Pilgrim Continues His Way*. Translated by R. M. French. San Francisco, CA: HarperSanFrancisco, 1991.

The *Way of a Pilgrim* is a mystical text of the Eastern Orthodox Church. It is more easily accessible than the *Philokalia* for those who want some background in Eastern Orthodoxy.

Brianchaninov, Ignatius. *On the Prayer of Jesus*. Boston, MA: New Seeds, 2006.

This book focuses specifically on explaining the methods and mysteries surrounding the Jesus Prayer. It is written from an Eastern Orthodox perspective and assumes knowledge of that context on the part of the reader.

Chumley, Norris J. *Mysteries of the Jesus Prayer: Experiencing the Presence of God and a Pilgrimage to the Heart of an Ancient Spirituality*. New York: HarperOne, 2011.

A wonderful beginner book for study of the Jesus Prayer and Eastern Orthodoxy generally. It is written from a Western Christian / secular perspective.

Goettmann, Alphonse, and Rachel Goettmann. *The Power of the Name: The History and Practices of the Jesus Prayer.* Rollinsford, NH: Orthodox Research Institute, 2008.

An invaluable historical and academic work on the Jesus Prayer. Please note that this is a book that is best for research, not practice.

Mathewes-Green, Frederica. *The Illuminated Heart: The Ancient Christian Path of Transformation.* Brewster, MA: Paraclete, 2001.

This is a great gateway book into Eastern Orthodox spirituality. Mathewes-Green has been associated with the emergent church, and she brings a more contemporary perspective to the study of spirituality here.

Mathewes-Green, Frederica. *Praying the Jesus Prayer: The Ancient Desert Prayer that Tunes the Heart to God.* Brewster, MA: Paraclete, 2011.

A great book to begin research into the Jesus Prayer. If you are not Eastern Orthodox, I suggest starting with *Praying the Jesus Prayer* or Chumley's *Mysteries of the Jesus Prayer* to go beyond my introduction to the practice in this chapter.

Ramon (Brother) and Simon Barrington-Ward. *Praying the Jesus Prayer Together.* Peabody, MA: Hendrickson Publishers, 2004.

The personal experiences of an Anglican monk and an Anglican bishop in praying the Jesus Prayer over the course of a week.

## Chapter 2: The Lord's Prayer

Ayo, Nicholas. *The Lord's Prayer: A Survey Theological and Literary.* Notre Dame, IN: University of Notre Dame Press, 1991.

Ayo provides an in-depth exegetical study of the Lord's Prayer along with commentary drawn from notable figures throughout the history of Christianity. This is an analytical work.

Boff, Leonardo. *The Lord's Prayer: The Prayer of Integral Liberation.* Maryknoll, NY: Orbis Books, 1983.

This is an interpretation of the Lord's Prayer through the lens of Liberation Theology, which interprets the life and teachings of Jesus in the context of social struggle.

Clark, David. *On Earth as in Heaven: The Lord's Prayer from Jewish Prayer to Christian Ritual*. Minneapolis, MN: Fortress Press, 2017.

Clark argues that the Lord's Prayer must be understood in the context of a revival of Jewish prayer forms in the first century. This book uses a historical-critical perspective.

Crosby, Michael H. *The Prayer That Jesus Taught Us*. Maryknoll, NY: Orbis Books, 2002.

A work that approaches the Lord's Prayer in a personal and devotional framework. Crosby also considers social justice aspects of the prayer.

Crossan, John Dominic. *The Greatest Prayer: Rediscovering the Revolutionary Message of the Lord's Prayer*. New York: Harper Collins, 2010.

Crossan considers the Lord's Prayer in the context of the search for the historical Jesus. This book is best for those who desire to study the Lord's Prayer from an academic perspective.

Gibson, Jeffrey B. *The Disciples' Prayer: The Prayer Jesus Taught in Its Historical Setting*. Minneapolis, MN: Fortress Press, 2015.

This work connects historical Jesus and social struggle themes. Gibson does not write on a devotional or personal level.

Maritain, Raïssa. *Notes on the Lord's Prayer*. New York: P. J. Kenedy & Sons, 1964.

A book of insightful meditations on the meaning of the Lord's Prayer. This book is written from an intellectual European Catholic perspective.

Oakman, Douglas E. *Jesus, Debt, and the Lord's Prayer*. Eugene, OR: Cascade Books, 2014.

This book considers the economic aspects of the role of debt within Jesus' teaching and uses the Lord's Prayer as the entry point for economic analysis.

O'Collins, Gerald. *The Lord's Prayer*. New York: Paulist Press, 2007.

An engaging first book to begin study of the Lord's Prayer from a Roman Catholic perspective.

Stevenson, Kenneth. *Abba, Father: Understanding and Using the Lord's Prayer*. Harrisburg, PA: Morehouse Publishing, 2000.

Stevenson writes this book as an engaging beginner book for a popular audience. He briefly considers biblical, theological, historical, and liturgical aspects of the prayer. This book is a great place to begin.

Stevenson, Kenneth. *The Lord's Prayer: A Text in Tradition*. London: SCM Press, 2004.

Stevenson approaches the Lord's Prayer from an academic scholarly perspective.

Tertullian, Cyprian, and Origen. *On the Lords' Prayer*. Translated by Alistair Stewart-Sykes. Crestwood, NY: St. Vladimir's Seminary Press, 2004.

Early church theologians' comments on the Lord's Prayer have been gathered and translated in this book.

Vinzent, Markus. *Meister Eckhart, 'On the Lord's Prayer': Introduction, Text, Translation, and Commentary*. Walpole, MA: Peeters, 2012.

Vinzent treats the role of the Lord's Prayer in the theology of the famous mystic Meister Eckhart. This book is not light reading.

Waetjen, Herman C. *Praying the Lord's Prayer: An Ageless Prayer for Today*, Harrisburg, PA: Trinity Press International, 1999.

This book has a direct devotional and practical focus in translating the Lord's Prayer into the terms and needs of Christians today.

Work, Telford. *Ain't Too Proud to Beg: Living through the Lord's Prayer*. Grand Rapids, MI: William B. Eerdmans, 2007.

This is an intensely practical book for using the Lord's Prayer in your life. I recommend beginning with either Wright or O'Collins, then following up with Work's book.

Wright, N. T. *The Lord and His Prayer*. Grand Rapids, MI: William B. Eerdmans, 1997.

An engaging first book to begin study of the Lord's Prayer from an Anglican perspective.

## Chapter 3: Lectio Divina

Benner, David G. *Opening to God: Lectio Divina and Life as Prayer*. Downers Grove, IL: IVP Books, 2010.

This book offers practical education in learning to use *lectio divina* from a veteran spiritual director.

Bianchi, Enzo. *Lectio Divina: From God's Word to Our Lives.* Brewster, MA: Paraclete Press, 2015.

Bianchi is a Christian monk, and he presents the history, theology, and practice of *lectio divina* within the monastic setting.

Casey, Michael. *Sacred Reading: The Ancient Art of Lectio Divina.* Ligouri, MO: Ligouri Publications, 1995.

A monastic-academic perspective of *lectio divina* is presented in this book. While steps of implementation are provided, the overall tone of the work is scholarly and research-focused.

Earle, Mary C. *Body Broken, Healing Spirit: Lectio Divina and Living with Illness.* Harrisburg, PA: Morehouse Publishing, 2003.

Earle provides a very personal reflection on the role that *lectio divina* can play in illness and recovery. This work presents a Christian perspective that pairs nicely with the many works on mindfulness and healing that come from a Buddhist or secular perspective.

Finley, James. *Christian Meditation: Experiencing the Presence of God.* San Francisco CA: HarperSanFrancisco, 2004.

This is a general work on all aspects of Christian meditation, which is Finley's term for the contemplative tradition in Christianity. It is a great place to continue your study after you begin using some of the practices presented in this book.

Hall, Thelma. *Too Deep for Words: Rediscovering Lectio Divina.* New York: Paulist Press, 1998.

Hall offers how-to methods for *lectio divina* coupled with five hundred scriptural texts for practice.

Johnson, Jan. *Meeting God in Scripture: A Hands-On Guide to Lectio Divina.* Oxford: Monarch Books, 2016.

In this introductory work on *lectio divina,* Johnson offers comments on method and unlike many other recommended books in this list, she offers interpretations for passages instead of leaving that matter up to the reader.

Kelsey, Morton T. *The Other Side of Silence: A Guide to Christian Meditation*. New York: Paulist Press, 1976.

This book offers theological and psychological insights into *lectio divina* and Christian spiritual practices generally.

Main, John. *Moments of Christ: The Path of Meditation*. New York: Continuum, 1998.

Main writes in a similar vein as Finley's *Christian Meditation*, but he has more emphasis laid on moving beyond techniques.

Paintner, Christine Valters, and Lucy Wynkoop. *Lectio Divina: Contemplative Awakening and Awareness*. New York: Paulist Press, 2008.

This is a thoroughly engaging work that balances history, theology, and practicality. I recommend starting with this book to go further with *lectio divina* beyond what I have written in this chapter.

Paintner, Christine Valters. *Lectio Divina--the Sacred Art: Transforming Words and Images into Heart-Centered Prayer*. Woodstock, VT: SkyLight Paths, 2011.

Paintner follows up *Lectio Divina: Contemplative Awakening and Awareness* with a more in-depth look into the practice.

Pennington, M. Basil. *Lectio Divina: Renewing the Ancient Practice of Praying the Scriptures*. New York: Crossroad, 1998.

Pennington, who is one of the founding fathers of centering prayer, presents *lectio divina* as the principal method to study scripture that pairs with the relatively wordless centering prayer practice (which is presented in chapter 8).

Pennington, M. Basil. *Living in the Question: Meditations in the Style of Lectio Divina*. New York: Continuum, 1999.

This book provides many entry points into *lectio divina* through common spiritual questions.

Studzinski, Raymond. *Reading to Live: The Evolving Practice of Lectio Divina*. Trappist, KY: Liturgical Press, 2009.

Studzinski writes a thoroughly historical work tracing the history and development of *lectio divina*. This book is more valuable for research than practical implementation.

von Balthasar, Hans Urs. *Christian Meditation*. San Francisco, CA: Ignatius Press, 1989.

This book presents the theological basis for God speaking to individuals in *lectio divina* and other Christian practices. It is a very difficult academic text from a premier twentieth-century Swiss theologian.

## Chapter 4: The Spiritual Exercises of St. Ignatius of Loyola

Barry, William A. *Finding God in All Things: A Companion to the Spiritual Exercises of St. Ignatius*. Notre Dame, IN: Ave Maria Press, 1991.

This book provides practical and thematic advice on using the spiritual exercises, particularly in contemplative retreats, from a veteran spiritual director. I recommend going to this book first if you want to go further than what I presented in this chapter.

Barry, William A. *Letting God Come Close: An Approach to the Ignatian Spiritual Exercises*. Chicago, IL: Jesuit Way, 2001.

Barry writes this book directly to retreat leaders and spiritual directors who want to facilitate Ignatian spiritual exercises for groups.

Becker, Ken. *Unlikely Companions: C.G. Jung on the Spiritual Exercises of Ignatius of Loyola: An Exposition and Critique Based on Jung's Lectures and Writings*. Leominster, UK: Gracewing, 2001.

This book is a cerebral engagement between the theology of Ignatius and the psychology of Jung. It is not light reading.

Cowan, Marian, and John Carroll Futrell. *Companions in Grace: A Handbook for Directors of the Spiritual Exercises of St. Ignatius of Loyola*. St. Louis, MO: Institute of Jesuit Sources, 2000.

Cowan and Futrell offer practical tips on the set-up and implementation of a religious retreat based on the spiritual exercises. This book is heavy on methodology rather than theory.

Dunne, Tad. *Spiritual Exercises for Today: A Contemporary Presentation of the Classic Spiritual Exercises of Ignatius Loyola*. San Francisco, CA: Harper San Francisco, 1991.

Dunne endeavors to update the Ignatian exercises for the modern spiritual seeker. The exercises often have difficulty coming across to a twenty-first-century religiously plural context instead of the six-teenth-century context of Christendom.

Fleming, David L. *Draw Me Into Your Friendship: A Literal Translation and a Contemporary Reading of the Spiritual Exercises*. St. Louis, MO: Institute of Jesuit Sources, 1996.

Fleming seeks to update the Ignatian exercises. Be aware that he takes the translation aspect very literally rather than more interpretively like Dunne.

Haight, Roger. *Christian Spirituality for Seekers: Reflections on the Spiritual Exercises of Ignatius Loyola*. Maryknoll, NY: Orbis Books, 2012.

This book provides introduction, context, and background for Ignatius of Loyola, the Society of Jesus, and the exercises. It is historical and academic rather than devotional and practical.

Helm, Nick. *Ignatius of Loyola: A Guide for Spiritual Growth and Discipleship*. Cambridge, UK: Grove Books, 2014.

Helm provides a very brief (twenty-eight pages) introduction to Ignatius and his exercises.

Horn, John. *Mystical Healing: The Psychological and Spiritual Power of the Ignatian Spiritual Exercises*. New York: Crossroad Publishing, 1996.

This book looks at the psychological aspects of Ignatian spirituality and the exercises, primarily through the use of case studies.

St. Ignatius of Loyola. *The Spiritual Exercises.* Translated by Louis J. Puhl. New York: Vintage Books, 2000.

The actual spiritual exercises of St. Ignatius are available in this book. My version in this chapter is highly interpretive, so you may want to begin further research by going to the original source.

Pungente, John J., and Geoffrey Bernard Williams. *Finding God in the Dark: Taking the Spiritual Exercises of St. Ignatius to the Movies*. Boston, MA: Pauline Books & Media, 2004.

Pungente and Williams follow in the line of authors who seek to update the spiritual exercises for modern audiences. They use the medium of movies as a common touchstone for the popular reader.

Sheldrake, Philip. *The Way of Ignatius Loyola: Contemporary Approaches to the Spiritual Exercises*. St. Louis, MO: Institute of Jesuit Sources, 1991.

This is a good beginner book to the spiritual exercises from one of the premier current spiritual theologians of the Jesuit order.

## Chapter 5: Reframing

Greenland, Susan Kaiser. *Mindful Games: Sharing Mindfulness and Meditation with Children, Teens, and Families.* Boulder, CO: Shambhala, 2016.

Greenland offers many practical exercises to introduce children to mindfulness. This is a great workbook that is especially geared to parents and teachers of children ages five to fifteen.

Hanh, Thich Nhat. *The Miracle of Mindfulness: An Introduction to the Practice of Meditation.* Boston, MA: Beacon Press, 1987.

This book is one of the best introductions to the practice of mindfulness from a specifically Buddhist perspective.

Hanh, Thich Nhat. *Peace Is Every Step: The Path of Mindfulness in Everyday Life.* New York: Bantam Books, 1991.

While Hanh has written many, many books on mindfulness, this book offers some practical step-by-step advice on how to get started with various meditations arising out of that tradition.

Johnson, Will. *Aligned, Relaxed, Resilient: The Physical Foundations of Mindfulness.* Boston, MA: Shambhala, 2000.

Johnson investigates the physiological aspects of mindfulness. It is a research-based work that offers relatively little for implementing practices.

Kabat-Zinn, Jon. *Full Catastrophe Living: Using the Wisdom of Your Body and Mind to Face Stress, Pain, and Illness.* New York: Bantam Books, 2013.

This is the seminal work in the field of mindfulness in a Western secular and medical context. It is a very large book that deals with practice and research. Many case studies are also provided.

Kabat-Zinn, Jon. *Wherever You Go, There You Are: Mindfulness Meditation in Everyday Life.* New York: Hyperion Books, 1994.

Kabat-Zinn provides this book for anyone who might find *Full Catastrophe Living* a bit too imposing. I recommend going further with mindfulness practices with one of Kabat-Zinn's books.

Mace, Chris. *Mindfulness and Mental Health: Therapy, Theory, and Science.* New York: Routledge, 2008.

This book concentrates on medical and psychological research, which demonstrates the objective effectiveness of mindfulness practices.

Shapiro, Shauna L., and Linda E. Carlson. *The Art and Science of Mindfulness: Integrating Mindfulness into Psychology and the Helping Professions.* Washington, DC: American Psychological Association, 2009.

Shapiro and Carlson present a well-researched argument for including mindfulness within all aspects of the American medical establishment. This work is the best one on this list for viewing mindfulness in a scientific, nonreligious context.

Siegel, Ronald D. *The Science of Mindfulness: A Research-Based Path to Well-Being, The Great Courses.* Chantilly, VA: Teaching Company, 2014. DVD.

This video series introduces the history, theory, and practice of mindfulness in a nonreligious (or non-Buddhist specific) context. It is a great resource for anyone who needs to see a practice in order to implement it.

Smalley, Susan L., and Diana Winston. *Fully Present: The Science, Art, and Practice of Mindfulness.* Cambridge, MA: Da Capo Lifelong, 2010.

This is a good general book introducing the use of mindfulness across multiple contexts.

Snel, Eline. *Sitting Still Like a Frog: Mindfulness Exercises for Kids.* Boston MA: Shambhala, 2013.

This book is a great resource for introducing mindfulness to children, and it includes an audio CD with guided meditations. Please note that Snel's book presupposes children to be older and calmer than Greenland's *Mindful Games.*

Wellings, Nigel. *Why Can't I Meditate: How to Get Your Mindfulness Practice on Track.* London: Piatkus, 2015.

Wellings offers a wonderful troubleshooting book for mindfulness practice. If you want the most directly practical path following what you have read in this chapter, then continue with Wellings.

Wilber, Ken. *Integral Meditation: Mindfulness as a Way to Grow Up, Wake Up, and Show Up in Your Life.* Boulder, CO: Shambhala, 2016.

This book combines mindfulness with philosopher Ken Wilber's Integral Theory. Step-by-step method is included with abstract theory and reinterpretation of our foundational assumptions. This book will definitely stretch your mind in new directions.

Zinser, Annabelle. *Small Bites: Mindfulness for Everyday Use.* Berkeley, CA: Parallax Press, 2012.

Zinser, a Buddhist teacher, offers practical meditations for using mindfulness in everyday settings and situations.

## Chapter 6: Observing

Refer to the titles listed for chapter 5 on pages 209–11.

## Chapter 7: Journaling

Adams, Kathleen. *Journal to the Self: Twenty-Two Paths to Personal Growth.* New York: Warner, 2009.

Adams provides multiple suggestions and recommendations for successful journaling for the purpose of personal development. This book is from a psychological perspective.

Atkinson, Robert. *The Gift of Stories: Practical and Spiritual Applications of Autobiography, Life Stories, and Personal Mythmaking.* Westport, CT: Bergin & Garvey, 1995.

Journaling can be approached from many different angles to develop your spirituality, but this is one of the few books that explores how creating one's own life story (i.e., "myth") can be a spiritual practice.

Baldwin, Christina. *Life's Companion: Journal Writing as a Spiritual Quest.* New York: Bantam, 1990.

This is a very practical book with lots of exercises to help you gain some experience and build the habit of journaling as a way to explore your own inner depths as opposed to journaling as a simple record of events of your day.

Cargas, Harry J., and Roger J. Radley. *Keeping a Spiritual Journal.* Garden City, NY: Doubleday, 1981.

This work is a bit dated, but it sets up the basic structure and step-by-step methodology for keeping a spiritual journal.

Comstock, Gary L., with C. Wayne Mayhall. *Religious Autobiographies.* 2nd ed. Belmont, CA: Thomson Wadsworth, 2004.

Comstock and Mayhall present many examples of effective spiritual journaling for religious purposes. No how-to methods are mentioned in this book.

Dixon, Janice T., and Dora D. Flack. *Preserving Your Past.* Garden City, NY: Doubleday, 1977.

This book guides you through the process of writing your own autobiography or family history. It does not approach journaling from an overtly spiritual perspective.

Klug, Ronald. *How to Keep a Spiritual Journal.* Minneapolis, MN: Augsburg, 1993.

Klug provides cogent and clear instruction in how to keep a spiritual journal along with the purpose, theory, and theology behind journaling as a spiritual practice. I recommend starting with this book if you want to go further with journaling than the introduction to the practice I offer here.

Mandelker, Amy, and Elizabeth Powers, eds. *Pilgrim Souls: A Collection of Spiritual Autobiographies.* New York: Touchstone, 1999.

A collection of many spiritual journals by religious role models offering examples and inspiration. This book does not contain how-to information on how to keep your own spiritual journal.

Phifer, Nan. *Memoirs of the Soul: Writing Your Spiritual Autobiography.* Cincinnati, OH: Walking Stick Press, 2002.

Phifer pens an engaging manual for how to write a spiritual autobiography. This work focuses principally on looking back over your life rather than chronicling events as they happen.

Pooley, Roger. *Spiritual Autobiography: A DIY Guide.* Bramcote, UK: Grove Books, 1983.

Pooley's book is a very brief introduction to spiritual journaling with focus only on the most essential pieces.

Santa-Maria, Maria. *Growth through Meditation and Journal Writing: A Jungian Perspective on Christian Spirituality*. New York: Paulist Press, 1983.

As the title suggests, this book approaches journaling form a Jungian perspective for utilization as a Christian spiritual practice. It is more psychological and theoretical than spiritual and devotional.

Scannell, Mark. *The Intensive Journal: Tapping the Creative Energy Within*. Minneapolis, MN: Sycamore, 1981.

Scannell writes a monastic perspective of spiritual journaling. This book was intended to accompany Intensive Journal workshops.

Vaughn, Ruth. *Write to Discover Yourself*. Garden City, NY: Doubleday, 1980.

Vaughn creates a guide on journaling for spiritual growth, but the real value of this work is her use and recommendation of the techniques of creative writing in the journaling process.

## Chapter 8: Centering Prayer

Bourgeault, Cynthia. *Centering Prayer and Inner Awakening*. Cambridge, MA: Cowley Publications, 2004.

Bourgeault presents a good overall treatment of the centering prayer practice and its ongoing popularity. She provides interesting avenues for the inclusion of centering prayer in all Christian institutional contexts.

Bourgeault, Cynthia. *The Heart of Centering Prayer: Nondual Christianity in Theory and Practice*. Boulder, CO: Shambhala, 2016.

This newer book by Bourgeault digs more deeply into the theory of centering prayer, and she places this practice against the backdrop of nondualistic thinking. This book is a good bridge between Far Eastern and Western ways of approaching spirituality.

Cassian, John. *Conferences*. Translated by Colm Luibheid. New York: Paulist Press, 1985.

Cassian's classic work introduces the practice of monasticism to the Western world through his many interviews and stories of the desert hermits who begin the Christian mystical tradition. This book is better for background of Christian contemplation than instruction in centering prayer.

Frenette, David. *The Path of Centering Prayer: Deepening Your Experience of God*. Boulder, CO: Sounds True, 2012.

This book is a good introduction to centering prayer from a student of one of the originators of the practice, Thomas Keating.

Keating, Thomas. *Divine Therapy and Addiction: Centering Prayer and the Twelve Steps*. New York: Lantern Books, 2011.

As the title of this book suggests, Keating compares, contrasts, and integrates centering prayer with the twelve-step program from Alcoholics Anonymous. This book is a must-read for anyone struggling with addiction in its various forms.

Keating, Thomas. *Open Mind, Open Heart: The Contemplative Dimension of the Gospel*. New York: Continuum, 2002.

This is a new edition of Keating's original work that introduced the centering prayer method. If you want to go further with centering prayer from what I have written here, then read this book along with Pennington's *Centering Prayer*.

Lawson, Paul David. *Old Wine in New Skins: Centering Prayer and Systems Theory*. New York: Lantern Books, 2001.

Lawson approaches centering prayer in its relationship with traditional psychological systems. It has a distinctly psychological framework for the presentation of centering prayer.

Muyskens, J. David. *Sacred Breath: Forty Days of Centering Prayer*. Nashville, TN: Upper Room Books, 2010.

This book offers a practical method for introducing centering prayer to churches and retreat groups. Most of the books on this list focus more on individual centering prayer, but Muyskens brings the group perspective to the forefront.

O'Madagain, Murchadh. *Centering Prayer and the Healing of the Unconscious*. New York: Lantern Books, 2007.

O'Madagain writes quite a bit about the history and provenance of centering prayer as well as its connections with psychology, especially

Jungian psychology. This should not be your first book on centering prayer because prior knowledge of the practice is presupposed.

Pennington, M. Basil. *Call to the Center: The Gospel's Invitation to Deeper Prayer*. Hyde Park, NY: New City Press, 1995.

Pennington follows up his magnum opus *Centering Prayer* with this smaller work as a taste of his thought and approach to contemplation.

Pennington, M. Basil. *Centering Prayer: Renewing an Ancient Christian Prayer Form*. Garden City, NY: Doubleday, 1980.

This is Pennington's comprehensive introduction to centering prayer. If you can only read one book about centering prayer, then this is the one to read.

Reininger, Gustave, ed. *Centering Prayer in Daily Life and Ministry*. New York: Continuum, 1998.

Reininger edits this collection of essays from pastors and priests who treat their use of centering prayer on personal and congregational levels. There are many ideas here for how to introduce this practice to churches.

Reininger, Gustave, ed. *The Diversity of Centering Prayer*. New York: Continuum Press, 1999.

This collection of essays relates the practice of centering prayer to other Christian practices and multiple different contexts for conceptual interpretation of centering prayer as experience.

Smith, Elizabeth, and Joseph Chalmers. *A Deeper Love: An Introduction to Centering Prayer*. New York: Continuum, 1999.

Smith and Chalmers provide a very brief introduction to centering prayer methods, summarizing Keating's writings and ideas.

Ward, Thomas R. *Centering Prayer*. Cincinnati, OH: Forward Movement Publications, 1997.

This particular book introduces the centering prayer method from the perspective and framework of a veteran spiritual director and contemplative retreat leader.

## Chapter 9: Clarity

See the titles listed for chapter 5 on pages 209–11.

## Chapter 10: Loving-Kindness Reflection

Buckley, Michael, comp. *The Catholic Prayer Book*. Edited by Tony Castle. Cincinnati: St. Anthony Messenger Press, 1986.

This book is a compilation of many traditional Catholic prayers from which I have pulled St. Patrick's breastplate as presented in this chapter. While the prayers in this book do not necessarily impact loving-kindness reflection, they can give voice to inchoate desires for sending out good thoughts to the world.

Also refer to the titles listed for chapter 5 on pages 209–11.

## Chapter 11: Letting Go

Foster, Richard. *Celebration of Discipline: The Path to Spiritual Growth*. Rev. ed. San Francisco, CA: Harper San Francisco, 1998.

Foster succinctly introduces several Christian mystical practices in relatable and practical terms. I have pulled and adapted the second variant of the "Letting Go" meditation from his chapter on meditation. Particularly if you come from an evangelical Christian background, *Celebration of Discipline* is a good place to start incorporating Christian mystic practices into your own spirituality.

Also refer to the titles listed for chapter 5 on pages 209–11.

## Chapter 12: Practicing the Presence of God

Brother Lawrence. *The Practice of the Presence of God with Spiritual Maxims*. Grand Rapids, MI: Spire Books, 1999.

This book is the primary source for understanding the practice of the presence of God, and it is a must-read for anyone interested in fully incorporating the practice into their lives.

de Caussade, Jean-Pierre. *The Sacrament of the Present Moment*. Translated by Kitty Muggeridge. New York: HarperOne, 1989.

De Caussade provides more theory behind this practice than Brother Lawrence. His book is invaluable for incorporating the practice into a robust sacramental theology. Beware, however, that there is a strong anti-intellectual bias in de Caussade's little book.

Epperly, Bruce Gordon, and Katherine Gould Epperly. *Tending to the Holy: The Practice of the Presence of God in Ministry*. Herndon, VA: Alban Institute, 2009.

*Tending to the Holy* takes Brother Lawrence's original ideas and translates them into the contemporary work contexts of pastors, priests, and other ministers.

Green, Timothy Mark. *Never Alone: Practicing the Presence of God*. Kansas City, MO: Barefoot Ministries, 2005.

Green reinterprets the practice defined by Brother Lawrence for a lay audience with youth and young adults especially in mind.

Obbard, Elizabeth. *Life in God's Now: The Sacrament of the Present Moment: Jean-Pierre de Caussade's Self-Abandonment to Divine Providence for Everyone*. London: New City, 2012.

Obbard does the translation and reinterpretation work for de Caussade that Green and the Epperlys do for Brother Lawrence.

## Chapter 13: Sitting Meditation

Refer to the titles listed for chapter 5 on pages 209–11.

## Chapter 14: Stargazing

Refer to the titles listed for chapter 5 on pages 209–11.

## Chapter 15: Nonjudging

Refer to the titles listed for chapter 5 on pages 209–11.

## Chapter 16: The Rosary

Doerr, Nan Lewis, and Virginia Stem Owen. *Praying with Beads: Daily Prayers for the Christian Year.* Grand Rapids, MI: William B. Eerdmans, 2007.

Doerr and Owen expand further than I have done here on the use and development of Anglican prayer beads. They offer multiple recommendations for prayers to use with these beads based on scripture and passages from the Book of Common Prayer.

Gurri, Margarita. *Anglican Prayer Beads: Prayer for Joyful Journeys.* Dania Beach, FL: Joyful Rhythms, 2013.

This book offers a briefer and more pragmatic treatment of Anglican prayer beads than Doerr and Owen.

McGee, Teresa Rhodes. *Mysteries of the Rosary in Ordinary Life.* Maryknoll, NY: Orbis Books, 2007.

McGee introduces the various "mysteries" that accompany the Roman Catholic Rosary tradition including the joyful, sorrowful, and glorious mysteries along with the mysteries of light. The mysteries of light are a recent addition to the Rosary tradition and were composed by Pope John Paul II.

Miller, John D. *Beads and Prayers: The Rosary in History and Devotion.* London: Burns & Oates, 2002.

*Beads and Prayers* relates the history and theology of the Rosary. This book definitely tends toward the theoretical and academic over the devotional aspects of the practice. Its primary utility is for scholarly research.

Pennington, M. Basil. *Praying by Hand: Rediscovering the Rosary as a Way of Prayer.* San Francisco, CA: HarperSanFrancisco, 1991.

Pennington's introduction, or reintroduction, to the Rosary is part persuasive invitation and part personal story. His viewpoint couples the Rosary nicely with the more abstract practice of centering prayer. If you enjoy centering prayer but would also like to keep your hands busy as you pray, then pick up this book to blend the two practices.

Phalen, John. *Living the Rosary: Finding Your Life in the Mysteries.* Notre Dame, IN: Ave Maria Press, 2010.

This book delves deeply into the mysteries of meditation within the use of the Roman Catholic Rosary. Phalen and McGee approach the same subject, and either book will give you a good foundation for meditating on the mysteries.

Vincent, Kristen E. *A Bead and a Prayer: A Beginner's Guide to Protestant Prayer Beads*. Nashville, TN: Upper Room, 2013.

Vincent introduces the use of prayer beads for a specifically Protestant audience. She does not limit her treatment only to the prayers of the Rosary. Also, she provides instruction for how to make your own prayer beads.

Wills, Gary. *The Rosary*. London: Souvenir Press, 2006.

*The Rosary* is a comprehensive treatment of the spiritual practice from a voice outside of professional religious and monastic circles. As a result, the relatable language of this book is a commonsense account of the history, development, and purpose of the Rosary. If you have no prior experience with the Rosary, then this book is a good place to learn the basic theology of it beyond what I present in this chapter.

Winston, Kimberly. *Bead One, Pray Too*. New York: Morehouse Publishing, 2008.

Winston's book is the best place to start for making rosary beads. If you want to build your hands-on spiritual practice from the ground up, then this is the book for you. She doesn't go into great length about using prayer beads with the Rosary, so you might couple this book with Wills or Vincent as a start.

## Chapter 17: Praying with Icons

Andreopoulos, Andreas. *Gazing on God: Trinity, Church, and Salvation in Orthodox Thought and Iconography*. Cambridge, UK: James Clarke & Co., 2013.

This book is a deep engagement with the use of icons as connected to central doctrines of Eastern Orthodox Christianity: the Trinity, ecclesiology, and soteriology. Andreopoulos presupposes an Eastern Orthodox perspective and presents a theoretical and academic case for his theological conclusions. I advise against this book being the first one you read on icons.

Bulgakov, Sergiĭ. *Icons and the Name of God*. Grand Rapids, MI: William B. Eerdmans, 2012.

From the purview of Eastern Orthodox theology, a major twentieth-century voice concerning praying with icons articulates the traditional position. This book is an English translation of two seminal essays by the leading Russian Orthodox theologian in the first half of the twentieth century.

Forest, Jim. *Praying with Icons*. Maryknoll, NY: Orbis Books, 1997.

Forest describes the practice of "reading" an icon, or praying with an icon, for an audience that is not familiar with the practice or Eastern Orthodoxy in general. Both theoretical and practical viewpoints are considered here.

Giakalis, Ambrosios. *Images of the Divine: The Theology of Icons at the Seventh Ecumenical Council*. Boston, MA: Brill, 2005.

This highly technical work investigates the eighth-century church council that established the validity and permissibility of using icons within all Christian prayer and worship contexts.

Green, Mary E. *Eyes to See: The Redemptive Purpose of Icons*. New York: Morehouse Publishing, 2014.

Green introduces icons and situates them within the life of Christian spirituality for a non-Orthodox audience. She is a retired Episcopal priest and approaches the spiritual practice principally from that perspective.

John of Damascus. *Three Treatises on the Divine Images*. Translated by Andrew Louth. Crestwood, NY: St. Vladimir's Seminary Press, 2003.

This historical work recounts the official argument undergirding the use of icons that became official in the Seventh Ecumenical Council. The primary worth of this book is theological and philosophical, not practical.

Martin, Linette. *Praying with Icons*. Brewster, MA: Paraclete, 2011.

Martin's slim volume is a good entry point to the utilization of icons beyond what I provide in this chapter.

Mathewes-Green, Frederica. *The Open Door: Entering the Sanctuary of Icons and Prayer*. Brewster, MA: Paraclete, 2003.

Mathewes-Green brings a contemporary, postmodern viewpoint to the use and incorporation of icons in worship. She does advocate conversion to Eastern Orthodoxy in order to use this practice effectively and appropriately.

Nouwen, Henri. *Behold the Beauty of the Lord: Praying with Icons*. Notre Dame, IN: Ave Maria, 1987.

This book presents the practice, but, more importantly, Nouwen lays the emotional groundwork for meeting God through icons. I recommend reading this book next if you like what you have read in chapter 17.

Ouspensky, Leonid, and Vladimir Lossky. *The Meaning of Icons*. Translated by G.E.H. Palmer. Boston, MA: Boston Book & Art Shop, 1956.

Ouspensky and Lossky pen a highly theological and abstract work on the significance of icons in the life of the church, particularly the Russian Orthodox Church.

Pearson, Peter. *A Brush with God: An Icon Workbook*. Harrisburg PA: Morehouse Publishing, 2005.

This is the number-one book for learning how to "write" an icon. If you want to put your hands into your prayers, then start here.

Quenot, Michel. *The Icon: Window on the Kingdom*. Crestwood, NY: St. Vladimir's Seminary Press, 1991.

Quenot considers the role of the icon in history, and, as a result, this book is far more art-focused than most of the recommendations on this list.

Tsakiridou, Cornelia A. *Icons in Time, Persons in Eternity: Orthodox Theology and the Aesthetics of the Christian Image*. Burlington, VT: Ashgate, 2013.

This book presents the theology of the icon in Eastern Orthodoxy, and Tsakiridou is meticulously successful in drawing the reader to the intersection of abstract theology and current art theory. This is a highly theoretical treatment, and it probably should not be your first encounter with icons.

Visel, Jeana. *Icons in the Western Church: Toward a More Sacramental Encounter.* Collegeville, MN: Liturgical Press, 2016.

Visel argues in this book for icons to find a place in Western Christianity, particularly Roman Catholicism, by situating the spiritual practice in a comprehensive sacramental view of the world.

Williams, Rowan. *The Dwelling of the Light: Praying with Icons of Christ.* Grand Rapids, MI: William B. Eerdmans, 2004.

Williams can pack a lot of theological truth densely into small volumes. This book is no different. He grounds his consideration of the role of icons in a Christian's spirituality through specific consideration of a few common icons of Jesus.

Williams, Rowan. *Ponder These Things: Praying with Icons of the Virgin.* Brewster, MA: Paraclete Press, 2006.

In this book, Williams does for icons of Mary what he did for icons of Jesus in *The Dwelling of the Light.* Either of these books are a great entry point to "reading" or praying with icons beyond what I present in these pages.

Zelensky, Elizabeth, and Lela Gilbert. *Windows to Heaven: Introducing Icons to Protestants and Catholics.* Grand Rapids, MI: Brazos Press, 2005.

Zelensky and Gilbert introduce icons for a Protestant and Catholic audience, but their book leans very heavily on the Protestant side of that divide. This book also seems to be a little less certain of Orthodox patterns of thought than Forest, Green, and Nouwen.

## Chapter 18: Body Scan

Refer to the titles listed for chapter 5 on pages 209–11.

## Chapter 19: Mindful Eating

Refer to the titles listed for chapter 5 on pages 209–11.

## Chapter 20: Drumbeat

Refer to the titles listed for chapter 5 on pages 209–11.

## Chapter 21: Fasting

Baab, Lynne M. *Fasting: Spiritual Freedom Beyond Our Appetites*. Downers Grove, IL: InterVarsity, 2006.

Baab offers practical advice on fasting along with a basic structure for situating this practice into Christian belief, particularly evangelical Christian belief.

St. Basil the Great. *On Fasting and Feasts*. Translated by Susan R. Holman and Mark DelCogliano. Yonkers, NY: St Vladimir's Seminary Press, 2013.

This historical essay on the role of fasting comes from one of the great fathers of the Christian tradition. *On Fasting and Feasts* is invaluable for understanding the history of fasting, but it presupposes a context in which fasting is quite common. That factor makes it a bit difficult to apply directly today.

Berghuis, Kent. *Christian Fasting: A Theological Approach*. Richardson, TX: Biblical Studies Press, 2007.

*Christian Fasting* is a published dissertation that investigates the theology of fasting from an evangelical Christian viewpoint. This book is not light reading.

de Vogue, Adalbert. *To Love Fasting: The Monastic Experience*. Translated by J. B. Hasbrouck. Petersham, MA: St. Bede's, 1989.

De Vogue examines fasting within the monastic context in which this practice fits most seamlessly. While this book is not applicable on a wide scale, it does present the ideal of the practice that you can keep in mind as you adapt the practice to your own experience.

Foster, Richard. *Celebration of Discipline: The Path to Spiritual Growth*. 20th anniversary ed.. San Francisco, CA: HarperSanFranscisco, 1998.

Foster's classic work introduces many disciplines to a (Protestant) Christian context that has forgotten their own rich spiritual heritage. His chapter on fasting is particularly practical and helpful in how to incorporate successfully this practice into your own spirituality.

Gregory, Susan. *The Daniel Fast: Feed Your Soul, Strengthen Your Spirit, and Renew Your Body*. Carol Stream, IL: Tyndale House Publishers, 2010.

The "Daniel Fast" has become a very popular variant of the spiritual practice of fasting with the express purpose of coupling fasting and prayer in search of specific answers to specific questions. While there is less applicability for Catholic, Orthodox, and Anglican/Episcopal Christians, evangelical Christians will likely find this source invaluable. This book also provides some points of contact with fasting for nonreligious reasons.

Ryan, Thomas. *The Sacred Art of Fasting: Preparing to Practice.* Woodstock, VT: Skylight Paths, 2005.

Ryan offers a balanced interreligious perspective on the practice of fasting. This work is probably the best one to give you an even foundation within the spiritual practice beyond the introductory comments of which I provide here.

Smith, David R. *Fasting: A Neglected Discipline.* 2nd ed. London: Hodder & Stoughton, 1974.

A simple introduction to the practice is available in this book, but there is heavy emphasis on the biblical use of fasting. This book is also from an evangelical Christian perspective, carrying certain biases against other avenues for implementing fasting.

Towns, Elmer. *The Beginner's Guide to Fasting.* Ventura, CA: Regal Books, 2001.

Towns offers some good practical tips for fasting in this book. While this book is light on history and theory, it is helpful in simplicity and direct instruction.

Wallis, Arthur. *God's Chosen Fast.* Fort Washington, PA: Christian Literature Crusade, 1986.

This book is a succinct how-to guide with generous application to the biblical context. The only problematic feature, however, is the relative lack of consideration of historic Christian fasting between the biblical period and the present era.

## Chapter 22: Labyrinths

Artress, Lauren. *Walking a Sacred Path: Rediscovering the Labyrinth as a Spiritual Tool.* New York: Riverhead, 1995.

Artress introduces audiences to the history and implementation of the labyrinth. This book is a great balanced gateway into effective utilization of this practice. I recommend proceeding to this book after reading what I have written on labyrinths in this chapter.

Camp, Carole Ann. *Praying at Every Turn: Meditations for Walking the Labyrinth*. New York: Crossroad, 2006.

While this book does briefly introduce the mechanics of walking the labyrinth as a spiritual practice, Camp focuses chiefly on the potential meditations to mull over as you walk. There is more content for the practice here rather than structure of the practice.

Curry, Helen. *The Way of the Labyrinth: A Powerful Meditation for Everyday Life*. New York: Penguin Compass, 2000.

*The Way of the Labyrinth* is full of practical application and personal reflection by the author. This book is particularly successful in its treatment of the potential interfaith context of walking a labyrinth.

Ferré, Robert. *The Labyrinth Revival*. St. Louis, MO: One Way Press, 1996.

This book is primarily historical and personal in its consideration of the rising popularity of labyrinths in the last few decades of the twentieth century. Some points of implementation are included, but the value of this book is chiefly historical and research-oriented.

Hartwell-Geoffrion, Jill. *Christian Prayer and Labyrinths: Pathways to Faith, Hope and Love*. Cleveland, OH: Pilgrim, 2004.

Hartwell-Geoffrion has several small application-oriented guides to the labyrinth, each of which focuses on different nuances of the practice. This guide focuses intently on the intersections of contemplative prayer with the labyrinth.

Hartwell-Geoffrion, Jill. *Labyrinth and the Song of Songs*. Cleveland, OH: Pilgrim, 2003.

In this book, Hartwell-Geoffrion connects the practice of the labyrinth with the scriptural book that has been most used in the Christian mystical tradition.

Hartwell-Geoffrion, Jill. *Living the Labyrinth: 101 Paths to a Deeper Connection with the Sacred*. Cleveland, OH: Pilgrim, 2000.

If you like new possibilities and options for using a spiritual practice, as I do, then this is the book on the labyrinth you should read. Innovate. Experiment. Try.

Hartwell-Geoffrion, Jill. *Pondering the Labyrinth: Questions to Pray on the Path*. Cleveland, OH: Pilgrim, 2003.

This book is a compilation of different meditations on big ideas and questions for you to ponder as you enter the labyrinthine path.

Hartwell-Geoffrion, Jill. *Praying the Labyrinth: A Journal for Spiritual Exploration*. Cleveland, OH: Pilgrim, 1999.

Hartwell-Geoffrion begins her consideration of the labyrinth in this book, and it is a great introduction to the practice. If you want a specifically Christian treatment of the labyrinth, I recommend going on to this book after my introduction to the practice.

Jaskolski, Helmut. *The Labyrinth: Symbol of Fear, Rebirth, and Liberation*. Translated by Michael H. Kohn. Boston, MA: Shambhala, 1997.

Jaskolski draws together a masterful academic treatment of the labyrinth as symbol across history, literature, and multiple religious traditions. Please note that this book is intended for research, not practice.

Kern, Hermann. *Through the Labyrinth: Designs and Meanings over 5,000 Years*. New York: Prestel, 2000.

Historical and archaeological perspectives predominate in this academic work. It is not light reading.

Lonegren, Sig. *Labyrinths: Ancient Myths and Modern Uses*. Glastonbury, UK: Gothic Image Publications, 1996.

While there are practical tips for use and construction in Lonegren's book, the main thrust of this work is in scrutinizing the mysteries of the labyrinth and its origin.

Taylor, Jeremy. *The Living Labyrinth: Exploring Universal Themes in Myth, Dreams, and the Symbolism of Daily Life*. Mahwah, NJ: Paulist Press, 1998.

Taylor stresses mythological and psychological themes in this book. It is a heavily archetypal work, and best approached by a reader familiar with Carl Jung and Joseph Campbell.

Westbury, Virginia. *Labyrinths: Ancient Paths of Wisdom and Peace*. Cambridge, MA: Da Capo Press, 2001.

Westbury pens the best introduction to the labyrinth from an overtly nonreligious perspective.

## Chapter 23: Pilgrimage

Barnes, Ruth, and Crispin Branfoot, eds. *Pilgrimage: The Sacred Journey*. Oxford, UK: Ashmolean Museum, 2006.

This book is a very broad-based introduction to the concept of pilgrimage across the three Abrahamic faiths: Judaism, Christianity, and Islam.

Bartholomew, Craig, and Fred Hughes, eds. *Explorations in a Christian Theology of Pilgrimage*. Aldershot, UK: Ashgate, 2004.

This is an anthology, and each essay considers deeply an aspect of Christian theology in direct comparison with the spiritual practice of pilgrimage, which has had an uneven history among different branches of Christianity. This book is very theoretical with few, if any, direct practical applications.

Bradley, Ian. *Pilgrimage: A Spiritual and Cultural Journey*. Oxford, UK: Lion Hudson, 2009.

Historical and theological in tone, Bradley writes an in-depth treatment of the practice of pilgrimage in the style of a college textbook.

Clift, Jean Dalby, and Wallace B. Clift. *The Archetype of Pilgrimage: Outer Action with Inner Meaning*. New York: Paulist Press, 1996.

The Clifts connect the spiritual practice of pilgrimage with the psychology of Carl Jung. This is a great place to begin if you are interested in psychological applications of pilgrimage.

Coleman, Simon, and John Elsner. *Pilgrimage: Past and Present in the World Religions*. Cambridge, MA: Harvard University Press, 1995.

Pilgrimage is another academic look at the subject, but this perspective is chiefly sociological and anthropological rather than theological and historical. It is one of the most interreligious works on the list.

Davies, J. G. *Pilgrimage Yesterday and Today: Why? Where? How?* London: SCM Press, 1988.

A primarily historical work, this book considers the history of pilgrimage in-depth, and it is particularly notable for including a lengthy section examining why Protestants rejected pilgrimage when they first separated from Roman Catholicism.

Eade, John, and Michael Sallnow, eds. *Contesting the Sacred: The Anthropology of Christian Pilgrimage.* Nashville, TN: Abingdon Press, 1991.

Multiple essays in this anthology deal with sociological and anthropological questions raised by the practice of pilgrimage in modern times. If you are interested in researching the intersections of globalism, tourism, and religious pluralism, then this is the book for you.

Forest, Jim. *The Road to Emmaus: Pilgrimage as a Way of Life.* Maryknoll, NY: Orbis Books, 2007.

Forest writes his personal reflections on the practice of pilgrimage and his many travels. If you desire a personal touchstone to understand an abstract practice, you might want to continue to this book after my introduction.

Harpur, James. *The Pilgrim Journey: A History of Pilgrimage in the Western World.* Oxford, UK: Lion Hudson, 2016.

The most comprehensive historical treatment of the spiritual practice of pilgrimage on this list of recommendations. It does not include much for application and implementation.

Harpur, James. *Sacred Tracks: 2000 Years of Christian Pilgrimage.* Berkeley, CA: University of California Press, 2002.

Harpur brings his keen historical eye to specifically Christian pilgrimage in this book.

Maddrell, Avril, Veronica della Dora, Alessandro Scafi, and Heather Walton. *Christian Pilgrimage, Landscape and Heritage: Journeying to the Sacred.* New York: Routledge, 2015.

This book offers a rare investigation of the role of landscape and geography in the development of the spiritual practice of pilgrimage. Collected essays present meticulous research from a scholarly perspective. This anthology requires background in the academic study of religion for the fullest possible understanding.

Reader, Ian. *Pilgrimage: A Very Short Introduction*. Oxford, UK: Oxford University Press, 2015.

While academic in nature, the very short introduction series provides a strong foundation for examining difficult issues in history and philosophy. The pilgrimage volume follows in the same general mindset. If you want to study pilgrimage from an academic perspective, this book is the best place to start.

Robinson, Martin. *Sacred Places, Pilgrim Paths: An Anthology of Pilgrimage*. London: Fount, 1998.

Robinson's work draws together primary sources on pilgrimage by pilgrims throughout the history of this spiritual practice. Multiple perspectives proliferate to give you a good sense of the diversity present in this practice and its role in differing religious traditions.

Sheldrake, Philip. *Spaces for the Sacred: Place, Memory, and Identity*. London: SCM Press, 2001.

Sheldrake considers the role of place in spirituality. This book is not solely about pilgrimage, but it does offer insight into a closely related area of religiosity. For pilgrimage to have meaning, place itself must have a spiritual connection.

Wright, Tom (N. T.). *The Way of the Lord: Christian Pilgrimage Today*. Grand Rapids, MI: William B. Eerdmans, 1999.

This brief introduction to Christian pilgrimage is the most concise and applicable book to the spiritual practice of which I am aware. Wright is widely known as having an engaging reading style, which is rare among theologians.

## Chapter 24: Body Flow: Pilates with Mindfulness

Bowen, Suzanne. *10-Minute Solution: Pilates Perfect Body*. S.I.: Anchor Bay Entertainment, 2009. DVD.

This video is a great, easy-to-follow exercise routine for Pilates. It has the added benefit of customization through choosing any one or more of five different Pilates routines in any combination of length in ten-minute increments.

Friedman, Philip, and Gail Eisen. *The Pilates Method of Physical and Mental Conditioning*. New York: Viking Studio, 2005.

If you are having difficulty understanding my descriptions of the Pilates movements, then you might proceed to this book. Friedman and Eisen provide many more pictures and in-depth descriptions of the exercises in their book.

Kries, Jennifer. *Pilates Plus Method: The Unique Combination of Yoga, Dance, and Pilates*. New York: Warner Books, 2001.

Kries'book starts off for beginners, but it quickly progresses to the advanced levels of physical activity. I recommend this book for any athletic individuals who find my variations on the exercises to not be challenging enough.

McGee, Kristin. *MTV Pilates*. Hollywood, CA: Paramount, 2004. DVD.

You don't have to like MTV to enjoy this workout routine. The main Pilates workout on the video covers most of the original exercises, so this video is ideal for visualizing what I describe in this chapter. McGee's version of the workout is also fairly brief. It will only take you about forty minutes to complete the entire series, which combines my three series, although in a different order of exercises.

McGee, Kristin. *MTV Pilates Mix*. Hollywood, CA: Paramount, 2004. DVD.

This video combines the ease of McGee's *MTV Pilates* with the options present in Bowen's video. As a personal word of warning, I have often hurt my back when I attempted to do a couple advanced variations of these Pilates'movements. This is not a beginner routine.

McKenzie, Eleanor, and Trevor Blount. *The Joseph H. Pilates Method at Home: A Balance, Shape, Strength, and Fitness Program*. Berkeley, CA: Ulysses Press, 2000.

McKenzie and Blount offer the closest interpretation to Pilates'original exercises other than his own books.

Pilates, Joseph H. *A Pilates' Primer: The Millennium Edition, includes the Complete Works of Joseph Pilates*. Ashland, OR: Presentation Dynamics, 2010.

Here is the original source, and I still think that it is well worth buying. Beware, however, that his explanation of the theoretical parts of his system is quite dated. The science of physical development has come a long way since the 1930s and 1940s.

Siler, Brooke. *The Pilates Body*. New York: Broadway Books, 2000.

Siler's book may be helpful to you if you desire to go beyond the basic mat exercises. She delineates many exercises that Pilates developed later in life in his exercise studio that needed specific apparatuses to perform.

Stewart, Kellina. *Pilates for Beginners*. New York: Harper Collins, 2001.

If you have never done anything with Pilates and you are uncertain about your physical fitness levels, then you would probably like to start with this book to ease into things. Please note, however, that you should consult your primary care physician before doing so.

See also the titles by Will Johnson, Jon Kabat-Zinn, and Annabelle Zinser listed under the resources for chapter 5 on pages 209–11.

## Chapter 25: Body Flow: Yoga with Centering Prayer

Dechanet, Jean. *Christian Yoga*. Translated by Roland Hindmarsh. New York: Harper & Row, 1960.

This is the original book that introduced the concept that yoga and Christianity could be compatible and that both traditions could benefit from that connection. Dechanet focuses on theory and personal reflection over description of poses. Also, he deals with an overtly religious form of yoga since nonreligious Western forms of yoga had yet to develop.

Dechanet, Jean. *Yoga and God*. Translated by Sarah Fawcett. St. Meinrad, IN: Abbey Press, 1975.

Dechanet expanded his original *Christian Yoga* with multiple other volumes throughout his life. In *Yoga and God*, he tackled the theological questions and difficulties of the relationship.

Dechanet, Jean. *Yoga in Ten Lessons*. Translated by S. F. L. Tye. New York: Harper & Row, 1965.

*Yoga in Ten Lessons* is the most practical of Dechanet's works, but it does not delineate a particular set of poses as much as articulate an attitude to approach life. There are many recommendations for effective breathing techniques in this work.

Hudson, Lara. *10-Minute Solution: Yoga*. Troy, MI: Anchor Bay Entertainment, 2005. DVD.

This video has the same benefits as delineated concerning the Pilates video in the series. You can customize in any of five directions of ten-minute increments. Some of these options are gentle and meditative; others are more vigorous.

Keating, Thomas. *Open Mind, Open Heart: The Contemplative Dimension of the Gospel*. New York: Continuum, 2002.

This is a new edition of Keating's original work that introduces the centering prayer method. If you want to go further with centering prayer from what I have written here, then read this book along with Pennington's *Centering Prayer*.

Matus, Thomas. *Yoga and the Jesus Prayer Tradition: An Experiment in Faith*. New York: Paulist Press, 1984.

Matus'book might seem to be a bit off-topic here since it considers the Jesus Prayer in relation to yoga, but it runs along very similar lines to what I have done in this chapter. Also, the Jesus Prayer is a short repetitive prayer, which serves an analogous purpose to the sacred word of centering prayer. This source might be a good one to stretch yourself with if you find that you like combining yoga and prayer.

McGee, Kristin. *MTV Yoga*. Hollywood, CA: Paramount, 2002. DVD.

You don't have to like MTV to enjoy this workout. McGee presents a balanced yoga flow that will give you an idea of how the poses are intended to flow one into the other. She does pick up the pace quite a bit from what I recommend. Many times where I recommend ten to twenty breaths she only recommends one. Fewer breaths direct the practice more toward the physical instead of the contemplative.

Pennington, M. Basil. *Centering Prayer: Renewing an Ancient Christian Prayer Form*. Garden City, NY: Doubleday, 1980.

This is Pennington's comprehensive introduction to centering prayer. If you can only read one book about centering prayer, then this is the one to read.

Roth, Nancy. *An Invitation to Christian Yoga*. New York: Seabury Books, 2005.

Roth offers a gentle introduction to Christian meaning tied to yoga movement in a similar way to what I have done in this chapter. If you want more of the same of what you have read here, then that might be the next book on the subject for you.

Slade, Herbert. *Exploration into Contemplative Prayer*. New York: Paulist Press, 1975.

Slade's book is the best discussion of theory and practice in combining yoga and contemplative prayer in a way that honors the traditions and values of both. I highly recommend this book for anyone interested in proceeding further in a combination of centering prayer and yoga.

St. Romain, Philip. *Kundalini Energy and Christian Spirituality: A Pathway to Growth and Healing*. New York: Crossroad, 1991.

This book approaches the convergence of traditions from the side of yoga. The other works in this list tend to come from the Christian side. It is highly technical concerning yoga theory and sophisticated breath techniques. I recommend that seasoned yoga practitioners only consult this book